The Tombigbee Watershed in Southeastern Prehistory

NED J. JENKINS
RICHARD A. KRAUSE

The Tombigbee Watershed in Southeastern Prehistory

THE UNIVERSITY OF
ALABAMA PRESS

Publication of this book has been made possible in
part by assistance from the Katherine Kreutner Campbell
Memorial Fund.

Library of Congress Cataloging in Publication Data

Jenkins, Ned J.
  The Tombigbee watershed in southeastern prehistory.

  Bibliography: p.
  Includes index.
  1. Indians of North America—Tombigbee River
Valley (Miss. and Ala.)—Antiquities. 2. Indians
of North America—Mississippi—Antiquities.
3. Indians of North America—Alabama—Antiquities.
4. Tombigbee River Valley (Miss. and Ala.)—
Antiquities. 5. Mississippi—Antiquities.
6. Alabama—Antiquities. I. Krause, Richard A.
II. Title.
E78.M73J46   1986   976.1′201   85-20879
ISBN 0-8173-0281-6 (alk. paper)

To the memory of
Steve B. Wimberly

Contents

Figures and Tables

Figures

Tables

Preface

The Tombigbee Watershed in Southeastern Prehistory is a synthesis of approximately ten years of archaeological field research along the central Tombigbee River. The issues raised by the synthesis have, however, been with us much longer. They include many problems basic to archaeological research throughout North America and some essential for general social inquiry. Among the former are (1) the logical and epistemological pitfalls inhering in the perennial quest for a workable systematics and (2) the always troublesome questions of the origin, spread, and adaptive significance of specific manufacturing, ritual, and economic practices. Among the latter are (1) the circumstances and forces which produce differentials in the command over resources and benefits among and within populations and (2) the overall end to which the trends and trajectories in social development may or may not be leading. These issues are joined here but are by no means unequivocally resolved. A final resolution lies beyond our competence. In addressing the issues we merely hope to produce a clearer understanding of what they are and why they vex us so.

The taxonomic ideas in our synthesis were born in the early 1960s in conversations with Irving Rouse. They were subsequently refined through course work with Rouse, Michael Coe, and Kwang Chi Chang. Those which survived matured in the mid-1960s under the skeptical and always demanding scrutiny of Preston Holder and in the late 1960s were forged in the heat of argument with Donald Lehmer, Raymond Wood, Alfred Johnson, and Carlyle S. Smith. They were reshaped in the light of southeastern archaeology through discussions with Christopher Pebbles, Eugene Futato, Carlos Solis, Vernon J. Knight, Jr., Vincas Steponaitis, Craig Sheldon, John Cottier, Rodger Nance, Reid Stowe, and Caleb C. Curren, Jr.

While we have done our best to provide a logically consistent taxonomic structure for ordering the data at our command, our taxonomic proposals should by no means be considered a final word on the subject. They are intended as interim measures to be revised, reworked, or discarded as more and better information becomes available. We view them as taxonomic hypotheses to be subject to the scrutiny of future field and laboratory tests. Some may stand the test of time, adequacy, and utility; others, we suspect, may not. Then too, it must be remembered that taxa are classes and taxonomic orders are logical orders, nothing more. Our taxa were created by definition, and while we attempted to justify them by their logical fit with the phenomena for whose study they were created, each must be interpreted in the light of a specific body of theory. This we have also tried to do.

The data for our classification and synthesis were acquired through the massive cultural resource management program which accompanied the construction of the Tennessee-Tombigbee Waterway. This work, which documented an archaeological sequence of over two millennia, was funded through contracts with the U.S. Army Corps of Engineers and conducted by many institutions. We have profited accordingly. Of particular import, however, was the part of the program conducted by The University of Alabama's Office of Archaeological Research and funded through a series of contracts with the Mobile Office of the Corps of Engineers. Jerry Nielsen, senior archaeologist for the Mobile District, United States Army Corps of Engineers, not only administered this project for the corps but also contributed by idea and action to its completion. Carey B. Oakley, director of The University of Alabama's Office of Archaeological Research, believed that the project could be finished and persevered in the face of severe budget limitations to see that it was completed.

Last but not least we would like to thank the staff of the Department of Anthropology and the Office of Archaeological Research, who contributed to preparation of the final manuscript. Michael Murphy of the Department of Anthropology read and commented upon portions of the manuscript as did Vernon J. Knight, Jr., of the Office of Archaeological Research. They are not, however, to be held guilty for our mistakes. C. Earle Smith, chairman of the Department of Anthropology, secured the funds necessary for the graphics, and Beverly Curry of the department typed the first draft of the manuscript. Louise K. (Kemp) White and Jackie M. Redding of the Office of Archaeological Research typed the final copy of the manuscript and Katherine Neff-Krause proofed and edited it. Richard Marshall of Mississippi State University contributed the recreations of Woodland and Mississippian houses. We thank all of them for their aid.

The Tombigbee Watershed in
Southeastern Prehistory

1. Introduction

Taxonomic Concerns

In archaeology, as in other disciplines, there is a periodic need for synthesis; a need to assess the accumulated data and wring from them a semblance of order; a need to systematize. This need has been felt in various areas at various times. Kidder (1924) addressed it in the Southwest; Champe (1946), Lehmer (1971), and Wedel (1959), in the Great Plains; and Caldwell (1958), Ford (1936), Griffin (1952a), Phillips (1939), and Willey (1949), in the Southeast. To be sure, these scholars and others too numerous to mention were addressing the need on a regional, or areawide scale. This is as it should be. The syntheses they created have, by and large, stood the test of time. But as the number of practicing archaeologists increased, as new analytical techniques and practices proliferated, and as the volume of detailed data pertinent to understanding subareal and subregional events grew, the need for new, albeit more restricted, syntheses grew apace. In sum, what were formerly area or regional needs, and very real ones, are now subareal and subregional needs, which are no less real. What is also true is that subareal and subregional syntheses must be embedded in area or regional accounts so that they elucidate rather than obscure the local working out of broader events and processes. Subareal or subregional syntheses should thus be test sections against which the broader sweep of prehistory can be evaluated and understood.

Viewed in hemispheric perspective, for instance, and seen through broad spans of time, the record of change in the New World seems reasonably regular (see Willey and Phillips 1958). Big-game hunting and the lifestyle this

1

subsistence mode engendered preceded the use of a smaller, more scattered game source. Increases in the efficiency of hunting and collecting preceded a settled lifestyle and prepared the way for agricultural modes of production. Agriculture, in turn, set the stage for material productions of some degree of sophistication and complexity and for such social enterprises as state formation and empire building (Fagan 1980; Hester and Grady 1982, 321–422). Yet detailed comparisons of artifact inventories, burial practices, domestic and public architecture, subsistence and settlement patterns, reveal localized trends and trajectories which are of restricted duration. Here there may be stability in artifact style; there, remarkable variability. Here there may be stability in burial practices; there, rapid alterations. A shift from surrounds to ambushes may characterize the hunting practices in one region. Drives may be the dominant and persistent pattern in a region nearby. These are the materials of subareal and subregional synthesis. It is precisely the shorter-term trends and trajectories that subareal syntheses should elucidate. These shorter-term trends and trajectories most severely challenge archaeologists' imaginations and propel them to seek their cause or causes (see Buikstra 1976). In their search for meaning in the evidence provided by the peoples of the past, most archaeologists adopt classificatory procedures of one kind or another. In this respect we can be no different from the rest. Nevertheless, we want our classificatory procedures to be firmly based in a rational consideration of the range of taxonomic means available to us. In short we want to derive our selection of taxonomic procedures from the classificatory experience of our predecessors and to do so in an explicit way. This will require a prefatory examination of the rich Americanist tradition of archaeological systematics, to which we now turn.

Taxonomic Issues

Like Robert Dunnell (1971, 8), we shall construe systematics as "the procedures for the creation of sets of units derived from a logical system for a specified purpose." Thus, to understand our predecessors' efforts to achieve an appropriate and satisfying systematics, we must explore the purposes for which they created their classificatory units and seek an understanding of the logic they used. The first of these aims requires a cursory review of the broader field of anthropological inquiry within which American archaeology is embedded. The second requires an explication of the logical means our predecessors used to achieve their classifications. Be advised, however, that our purpose in conducting this inquiry is to provide ourselves with a springboard for determining our own classificatory and interpretative needs.

American archaeology has always been a part of anthropology, though much that is incorporated in it can be traced to a European tradition of scholarship which had its origin in the antiquarianism of the sixteenth to eighteenth centuries. In Europe an initial interest in antiquities was accommodated to the three-age system of Christian Jurgensen Thomsen, the geological ideas of Charles Lyell, and the demonstration of man's antiquity by Boucher de Perthes. In the last half of the nineteenth century and early years of the twentieth, the British produced techniques of excavation, analysis, and interpretation which set European archaeology on its separate course (Daniel 1967, 22, 45, 211–48). But Americans bonded elements of the European discipline to a tradition which was anthropological in organization and perspective, and for good reason. Our European colleagues had a rich body of records at their disposal; Americans, on the other hand, dealt with the remains of preliterate peoples whose chief testimony lay buried in the earth. Thus many archaeological finds in Europe could be interpreted in the light of written records, while the interpretation of Amerindian archaeological materials, for the most part, depended on recent ethnographic accounts or the potential inhering in contemporary ethnological theorizing.

In the last half of the last century, the focus of most ethnological inquiry was the evolutionary succession of social forms and technological orders that presumably marked the course of human history (e.g., Morgan 1877, Tylor 1871). An emphasis on the manufacture and use of artifacts as "traits" suitable for broad classificatory ends was embedded in this evolutionary perspective. Its most eloquent American proponent, Lewis H. Morgan (1877), saw certain social practices and the artifacts that were a part of them as markers of progress. The bow and arrow was considered a marker of the stage of Upper Savagery; pottery making an indicator of Lower Barbarism. Plant and/or animal domestication, irrigation, adobe and stone architecture, signaled the onset of Middle Barbarism, and iron tools, the emergence of Upper Barbarism. Civilization was accompanied by a phonetic alphabet and writing. Although the inadequacies of this approach have been widely discussed, Morgan's "general sequence of stages has been written into our understanding of prehistory and interpretation of archaeological remains, as a glance at any introductory text will indicate" (Leacock 1963, lxi).

In the late nineteenth century the idea of a world-embracing evolutionary order crumbled before the formidable assault of Franz Boas, who stressed field observation as a check on claims to knowledge (Boas 1948, 275). American anthropologists turned their attention to fieldwork and the creation of a restricted and explicitly historical interpretive format (Harris 1968, 250–372). As fieldwork blossomed, ethnographic collections in American museums grew, together with an emergent antievolutionism, which fostered the idea of using geographic categories as display units. The first public statement of this trend occurred in 1895 when Otis T. Mason (1896), in a lecture at the

Smithsonian Institution, proposed a scheme which implied isomorphism among native cultures in a region. Vastly different schemes were proposed by C. Thomas (1898) and by McGee and Thomas (1905), but Mason's view survived and prospered.

While the culture area idea owed its origin to the problems of museum displays, it was soon used to meet the needs of ethnological theory building. Mason's culture areas were modified by Holmes (1914) in the early years of the twentieth century and became central to Wissler's (1917) work in American Indian ethnology. Shortly thereafter, the idea became "a community product of nearly the whole school of American anthropologists" (Kroeber 1931, 259). An ethnographic map which grouped societies by proximity and similarity in aspects of environment and culture had empirical appeal. The emphasis was still on culture traits, but these were now arranged in a spatially documented rather than a temporally speculative order. Kroeber's (1939) culture areas of the 1920s were created from sizable lists of traits, an approach which reached its logical extreme in the University of California's survey lists of 3,000 to 6,000 items (Kroeber and Driver 1932).

Insofar as culture areas were construed as self-contained, geographically and culturally homogeneous regions without temporal boundaries, the explanatory value of the approach was limited. But if temporal order was to be inferred, as in the age-area hypothesis, or if inter- or intra-area comparisons were necessary, there were empirical and epistemological problems (Harris 1968, 375–77). Despite the recognized inadequacies of culture area formulations, they directed attention to the limitations and potentials of a trait list approach and focused interest on the significance of man-technology-land relationships. They were the precursors of attempts to form content-based taxonomies like the Midwestern Taxonomic System and to subdivide areas and regions into taxonomically meaningful spatial units like those proposed by Willey and Phillips (see McKern 1939 and Willey and Phillips 1958).

As American ethnologists struggled with the problems of the culture area their archaeological counterparts created their own versions of a "more restricted and explicitly historical interpretative format" (see Taylor 1948, 24). A two-part program of archaeological inquiry emerged; one part devoted to working from the recent and documented past to the prehistoric past, the other to arranging taxonomically created units in chronological order. Practitioners of the first approach argued that if historically documented sites could be located and a suitable archaeological sample drawn and analyzed, then (within certain limits) an ethnic identity could be assigned to co-occurring ceramic styles, house types, burial practices, and tool technologies (see Dixon 1913, 549–77; Myer 1922; and Wedel 1936 for examples). Further, once properly attributed to an ethnic group, a recurrent complex of such elements could be used to identify protohistoric and prehistoric villages and camps, thus giving spatial and temporal substance to historically documented cultures (see Mott 1938, Strong 1940, and Wedel 1936). This "direct historic approach" seems to have lapsed, imperceptibly perhaps, into the practice of labeling spatially and temporally restricted prehistoric element complexes as cultures despite the fact that the historical documentation needed to do so was lacking (see Gilder 1907 and 1926 for examples). The ultimate goal, of course, was to link these prehistoric "archaeological" cultures to their historic counterparts, thus providing a contextual history of considerable precision, interest, and interpretive power.

It soon became obvious, however, that the congruity between historically distinct ethnic groups and their material remains was far from exact, so much so in fact that many interpretive problems could not be dismissed as the expectable consequences of sample size, context control, or the selection of analytical ideas and techniques. There were a few notably successful attempts to link historic with protohistoric remains (Strong 1935, Wedel 1936), but the more ambitious efforts to tie the materials of history to those of prehistory were, by and large, unsuccessful. Precision in building a contextual history was to be sought elsewhere, and most, if not all, American archaeologists directed their attention to the creation of classificatory units which focused upon the material remains themselves rather than upon the ethnic identity that could be imputed to them. For these scholars, archaeology became the systematic study of the distribution of prehistoric objects in time and space. Foci, phases, or archaeological cultures, devoid of ethnic or social connotations, became the subjects of analytical inquiry, and correlating these units in time and space became the sine qua non of archaeological interpretation (Taylor 1948, 53). Culture history, as this approach came to be called, stressed systematic attempts to order archaeological complexes into local and regional sequences (Willey and Sabloff 1974, 64). For this endeavor changes in the popularity of artifact types, modes, attributes, or combinations of the three were deemed important for inferring the temporal relatedness of various cultures, phases, or foci (Phillips, Ford, and Griffin 1951; Rouse 1939; Spaulding 1956). To its critics, however, culture history had the interpretive potential of a series of artifacts strung on the clothesline of time (see Binford 1962 and 1965 for examples). There was a kind of subject-object identity in this approach that many archaeologists found intellectually debilitating.

With the mid-twentieth-century advent of the "new archaeology" (however appropriate this label may be), artifactual data were used to make inferences about the structure of extinct cultural systems (Kushner 1970, 125). Deetz (1965), for instance, suggested that changes in ceramic attribute clustering reflected changes in Arikara postnuptial residence choices, and Binford (1965) argued that modifications of artifact inventory sometimes indicated alterations in the size, composition, and organization of domestic groups.

Longacre (1970) used the distribution of ceramic types together with other data to draw a picture of sociological divisions in a prehistoric pueblo. These, and many other works, reflected a growing interest in the capacity to infer kinship and residence practices and social, political, and economic institutions from an analysis of the spatial and temporal distribution of artifacts. These were challenging attempts to supersede the subject-object identity that seemed to guide prevailing studies of culture history, but their explanatory power was constrained by a static perspective that seemed necessary if artifact kind, quantity, and distribution contrasts were to be correlated with social forms or practices. In fact, a static bias was so thoroughly and seductively embedded in the "new archaeology" that (without either difficulty or much additional work) analysts achieved a less than dynamic view of the phenomena whose origins and development they ultimately sought to understand.

Recent practitioners of archaeological science have expressed a greater concern for the study of social dynamism, and some have attempted to transform the static perspective inhering in the new archaeology to a morphogenetic view—a view in which time- and/or space-persistent continuities in artifact manufacture and use are actively sought as the objects of explanation (see van der Leeuw 1982, 431–57). This morphogenetic view has a dynamism which springs from stressing the constant generation of acts, events, and processes from previous contexts. What happens when this perspective is applied is that the search for continuity (and its complement, discontinuity) serves as a springboard for explanation attempts which have recourse to a preexisting body of theory. Thus it is a preexisting body of theory which constitutes the subject of inquiry and which leads the archaeologist to anticipate those continuities and discontinuities that are to be the objects of study. These processualists, as some have called themselves, have, in effect, placed the new archaeologists' interest in principles of social order in a theory-dependent developmental perspective.

Both the processualists and the new archaeologists before them tied their efforts to a taxonomic apparatus initially developed for the study of culture history. This is certainly an understandable, if not an inevitable, turn of events. The fusion of new interests with taxonomic procedures devised for other and, in some cases, incompatible ends is reasonably common and often productive. The fusion in this particular case has, however, been an inexplicit, incomplete, and in some ways an uncomfortable one. Indeed, at least some of the problems faced by proponents of processualism are consequences of this fusion. Processualists have yet to explore adequately the logical limitations and potentials inhering in the taxonomic procedures originally designed for the study of culture history. To illustrate why a concern for social process might require a modification of these procedures, we shall discuss the logic underpinning two of them—the Midwestern Taxonomic System (M.T.S.) and the Willey and Phillips Phase-Tradition-Horizon system.

The Midwestern Taxonomic System

The Midwestern Taxonomic System is a six-taxon, content-based form of data arrangement based on the logical principle of strict set inclusion (Kay 1971, 868). Component, focus, aspect, phase, pattern, and base are included as taxa (McKern 1939, 301–13), but for convenience most users restrict the system to component, focus, and aspect (Hurt 1953, Stephenson 1954). These taxa are arranged so that each lower-level unit is a proper subset of one (and only one) higher-level unit. A component, for instance, can be a member of only one focus, and a focus can be a member of only one aspect (fig. 1). Thus the arrangement proceeds from taxa of greatest specificity and narrowest range (components) to those of least specificity and broadest range (foci and aspects) (Dunnell 1971, 177–83). Krause (1977) argues that components are to be construed as "kinds of" foci and foci as "kinds of" aspects. In explicating the expression "kind of," he notes that components are commonly considered manifestations of a focus at a single place and that foci are components sharing a preponderant majority of traits. An aspect, he continues, is customarily interpreted as a group of foci having a majority of traits in common. Thus, he concludes, a superficial inspection suggests that the number of trait replications (stated as a percent of the total) is a rough and ready indicator of position within the taxonomic hierarchy. From this he deduces that "one important consequence of the M.T.S. is the fact that the most inclusive units have the least replicated content and the least inclusive units have the most" (Krause 1977, 6).

All M.T.S. taxa are composed of traits (McKern 1939, 301–13), and although the archaeological and ethnographic literature is far from clear on this point, let us assume that the term *trait* designates a class of entities. Thus the

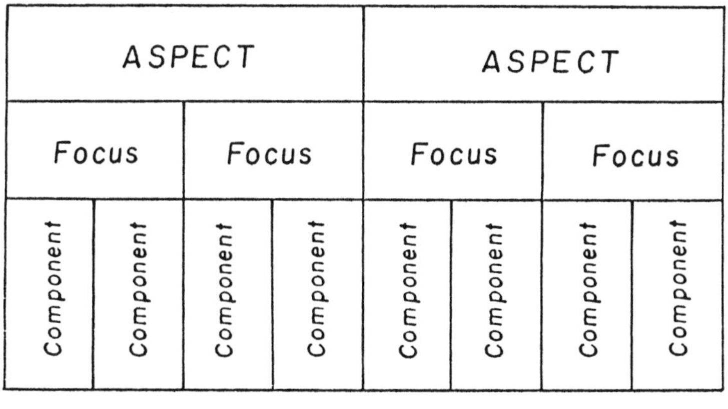

ASPECT				ASPECT			
Focus		Focus		Focus		Focus	
Component	Component	Component	Component	Component	Component	Component	Component

Figure 1. A Diagram of the Unit Relationships in the M.T.S.

trait "cord roughened exterior vessel surface" is an elliptical way of indicating one member of the class of all pottery vessels whose exterior surfaces have been malleated with a cord-wrapped paddle. Therefore to say that component A and component B share the trait "pottery with cord roughened exterior surfaces" is to argue that each of the two components has at least one member of the class of all cord-roughened exterior vessel surfaces. This allows us to understand the term *share* in a clear and logically precise way. By *share* we mean that each of two or more components contains at least one member of a non-component-specific class of objects or entities. Class and trait now become synonymous such that the archaeologist examining and analyzing an array of archaeological materials posits a series of classes identified as traits. Since the membership of a class is potentially infinite, the analyst may rightfully assume that additional members will be found at other sites or components and M.T.S. taxa may be formed by noting the number of classes having legitimate members at two or more components. It is, therefore, *the number of classes* with members at various components that provides the basis for calculating quantities such as majority, preponderant majority, and so on. To rephrase and summarize the issue, M.T.S. aspects should have fewer classes than foci, and foci should have fewer classes than components. Nevertheless, all the classes in an aspect must have members in the included foci and components, and all the classes in the focus must have members in the included components.

Time and space are a problem for the M.T.S. They cannot be handled with the same set-inclusive logic applied to content. If, for instance, we maintain a strict interpretation of *shared,* the time span of a focus would be those years, from each component, which were members of a common set or class of years. Thus if component A was occupied from 1400 to 1425, and component B from 1420 to 1450, there would be only five years common to the set of all years from 1400 to 1425 and only five years common to the set of all years from 1420 to 1450, yielding a logically legitimate duration of five years for the focus. This makes little, if any, empirical sense because ultimately the most inclusive taxa will have the shallowest logically permissible slice of time. Similar considerations apply to attempts to introduce space as a trait during taxon formation. McKern's (1939, 301–13) solution to this conundrum was to exclude both time and space from taxon formation. An alternative solution can be posed if we adopt a liberalized interpretation of *shared* by allowing a redefinition of the temporal or spatial reference class at each successively higher level of taxa formation (see Krause 1977, 5–8). If we allow reference class redefinition and posit for our previously introduced components A and B the set of all years from 1400 to 1450, we would have members at both components and could proceed to form higher-level taxa. We must remember, however, that our higher-level taxa must also be composed of classes with members in all the lower levels such that even if the set of all years from 1400 to 1450 may suffice for placing components A and B in the same focus, we have no reason to believe that the same set of years will be adequate for placing this focus in an aspect. This latter operation will almost certainly call for an additional redefinition of temporal reference class. Thus, the proposed solution, through multiple redefinition, is workable but a bit cumbersome. Nevertheless, if multiple redefinition is necessary, it should be obvious that the required redefinitions must be based on prior knowledge of the taxa deemed appropriate for inclusion in each higher-level taxon. In short, if the logic inhering in the M.T.S. is to be maintained, taxa must be formed on the basis of their content before a set of appropriate years or a specification of applicable space can be proposed. Thus the M.T.S. does not facilitate the mapping of content continuities, for to do so requires recourse to connectedness in time, in space, or in both. Since processual studies depend upon recognizing content continuities, the M.T.S. is a limiting rather than facilitating system for them. The same, however, is not true of the Willey and Phillips system (see Krause 1977, 5–13).

The Willey and Phillips System

The Willey and Phillips system is based upon a paradigmatic logic which incorporates time and space in taxa formation. The basic taxa in the system (the phase, tradition, and horizon) are created by the intersection of values along the dimensions of time, space, and content. Willey and Phillips (1958, 22) describe the relations among these units as follows: the phase is a classificatory taxon; the horizon and tradition are integrative taxa (fig. 2). Let us form the three taxa from the dimensions of time, space, and content by indicating a greater or lesser emphasis with a plus (+) or minus (−) sign, in which a plus sign means greater emphasis and a minus sign means lesser emphasis. This operation produces:

Dimensions		*Values*	
Time	T	Greater	(+)
Space	S	Lesser	(−)
Content	C		

such that their intersection yields

Phase	C+ · T− · S−
Tradition	C− · T+ · S−
Horizon	C− · T− · S+

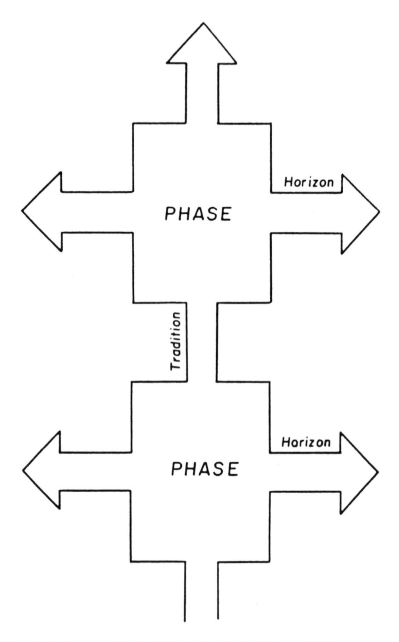

Figure 2. A Diagram of the Unit Relationships in the Willey and Phillips System

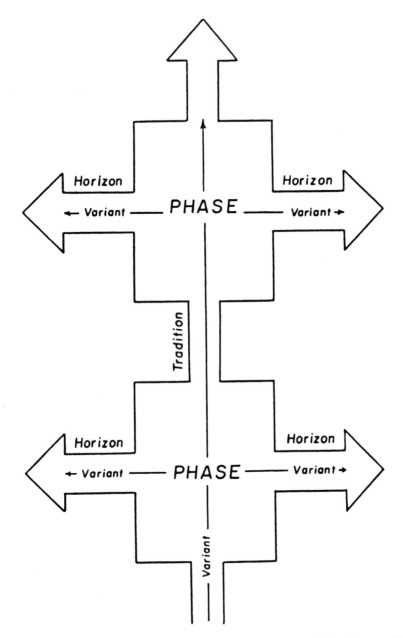

Figure 3. A Diagram of the Unit Relationships in the Willey and Phillips System with the Variant Added

Rearranging to display the classificatory principle at work gives

	Content	Time	Space
Phase	+	−	−
Tradition	−	+	−
Horizon	−	−	+

The following implications can be drawn from the intertaxa relations displayed above. To use the system adequately:

1. Phases must always have the greatest content.
2. Traditions must always have the greatest time depth.
3. Horizons must always have the greatest spatial spread.
4. Traditions and horizons may have roughly equal content but must have less content than any phase integrated by them.
5. Phases and traditions may have roughly equal spatial dimensions but must have less than any horizon which integrates them.
6. Phases and horizons may have roughly equal time spans but must be less durable than any tradition which integrates them.

In 1971 Lehmer (1971, 32) proposed a modification of the Willey and Phillips system by introducing the variant which he described as "a unique and reasonably uniform expression of a cultural tradition which has a greater order of magnitude than a phase and is distinguished from other variants of the same tradition by its geographic distribution, age and/or cultural content." In 1977 Krause (1977, 10) explicated Lehmer's use of variant and recast it as "a mid-range taxon which has less content, greater time span and greater spatial spread than a phase, but less time span than a tradition and less spatial spread than a horizon" (fig. 3). Thus construed, the variant fits securely within the paradigmatic logic of the Willey and Phillips system as indicated by:

Dimensions		Values	
Time	T	Greater	(+)
Space	S	Lesser	(−)
Content	C		

such that,

Phase	$C+ \cdot T- \cdot S-$
Variant	$C- \cdot T+ \cdot S+$
Horizon	$C- \cdot T- \cdot S+$
Tradition	$C- \cdot T+ \cdot S-$

The following is a way to display the schemata:

	Content	*Time*	*Space*
Phase	+	−	−
Variant	−	+	+
Tradition	−	+	−
Horizon	−	−	+

In sum, the M.T.S. is based upon a set inclusive logic; the Willey and Phillips Phase-Tradition-Horizon system, on a set intersective or paradigmatic logic. The paradigmatic logic of the Lehmer-modified Willey and Phillips system fits our needs best. It will therefore form the taxonomic backbone of our synthesis. It must, however, be understood that our comparison of the M.T.S. and the Willey and Phillips system is intended to underline the fact that they are different logical orders, nothing more, nothing less. Our intent is not to criticize. Rather it is to show that each taxonomic system has certain potentials and limitations which derive from the logical operations at its core. In other words, we construe both as pure logical systems devoid of empirical meaning. Such meaning as each achieves, it achieves through use, through the empiricization archaeologists give it as they struggle to understand the intellectual and artifactual materials at their command. Thus, while we have chosen the Willey and Phillips system as most compatible with our *logical* needs we consider its customary empiricization to be a separate issue and have chosen to recast this element in the light of our own aims. Be warned, therefore, that a satisfactory account of the meaning we assign to phases, variants, traditions, and horizons will not reflect customary usage but will instead depend upon the body of theory we have selected to guide our synthesis.

Toward an Interpretation of the Willey and Phillips System

In our synthesis we shall work within the general theory of evolution currently popular among archaeologists. This choice will limit us to seeking functional explanations for growth, loss, or fixation of variety in operationally defined systems. From this perspective, culture is considered a system; that is, it is viewed as an intercommunicating set of parts (subsystems or institutions), with human behavior as the analytically salient point of subsystem or, in our view, institutional articulation (for a similar point of view see van der Leeuw 1981 and 1982). Variation in human behavior must then be considered a product of institutional reorganization and a means for reestablishing disrupted systemic harmony. Disruptions are the products of external social, political, economic, or environmental pressures whose net effects exceed those tolerable by system internal balance-maintaining forces. Culture change is achieved through variation in one or more of the institutions which grows or is diminished in import, or which displaces or reinforces others (see Krause 1977, 10–13).

To use the culture as system approach, one must identify those internal forces maintaining balance and those external pressures promoting change. The major problem with this construal is its atomism, its propensity to see motion as a consequence of the interaction of two or more entities rather than an integral part of the system itself. There thus tends to be an emphasis upon being rather than becoming and upon structure rather than structuring (for a more detailed criticism see van der Leeuw 1982). We suspect that some of these analytical drawbacks may be softened (if they cannot be avoided) by interpreting external and internal forces as being at one and the same time both entities and flows of information, matter, and energy (see Prigogine 1978). But if we do so we must account for the fact that matter and energy are subject to the law of conservation, while information is not. Information is therefore analytically primary in the sense that it can be responsible for the creation and maintenance of potentials for dynamism, whereas energy and matter, in and of themselves, cannot.

Let us now agree that traditional knowledge about how things should be done is an essential balance-maintaining force. When construed as entities, traditional bodies of knowledge give shape and substance to institutions (sets of kinship ties, burial rituals, manufacturing techniques, subsistence practices, etc.). When construed as flows, they take the form of transgenerational inter- and/or intra-cultural idea exchange mechanisms (i.e., information routes or channels). Let us further assume that essential parts of a traditional body of knowledge can be understood through the analysis of artifacts and artifact by-products (i.e., that archaeologists can read from artifacts the traditional standards, customs, and beliefs which guided raw material acquisition, manufacturing steps, and forms of use). Finally, let us stipulate that system external forces can be interpreted as environmental whether they be social or natural. When construed as entities, system external forces take the form of usable resources (natural foods, climate, soils, timber, mineral deposits, etc.). When interpreted as flows, they may be seen as energy, matter, and information exchange networks (routes of trade and commerce, pathways of stimulus diffusion, or avenues of population growth and dispersal). System external forces can, therefore, be inferred from an understanding of the distribution of particular kinds of artifacts and artifact by-products.

The previously tendered stipulations may now be used to assign a fuller meaning to our construal of phases, variants, traditions, and horizons. We want phases to be intelligible units for studying the interplay among sociocultural variations and definable external forces. From our perspective the phases in a region should be logically congruent with system states. Further, if we construe components as synonymous with communities, phases are system states which express multicommunity information, matter, and energy exchange climaxes. They are entities which are the results of intense energy, matter, and information flows. Information, matter, and energy flows at the phase level are, however, funneled through social institutions which are more than mere conduits. These social institutions both constrain the flows and are shaped by them. Hence we expect a degree of variability among the components of a phase as the flows which give them their coherence wax and wane. Nevertheless, the spatial dimensions for a phase should fit with our understanding of the geographical maxima for maintaining intensity in energy and matter exchange at a given level of technology, and the temporal dimensions concur with our best judgment of intensity in information exchange as this can be read from similarities in the details of artifact manufacture and use.

If phases are to represent system states whose information, matter, and energy flows are constrained by institutions, then traditions may be interpreted as long-term, suprainstitutional information exchange routes that integrate system states in time. Put differently, traditions may be understood as time-ordered and durable sequences of artifact manufacture and use created by the unfolding of an underlying, albeit limited, body of knowledge. Traditions express the information contained in but a few of the technologies found in a given phase. Traditions seem free of the dissipative effects of most entropy-producing events and processes because they represent almost pure information. It is this aspect that gives them their long-term temporal force and makes them such efficient broad-range integrative tools. Further, it is the ideological and social constraints contained in the limited information-constituting traditions that give them a conservative force, a persistence against which the dynamics of other energy- and matter-constrained bodies of knowledge may be profitably understood.

Horizons may be construed as roughly synchronic suprainstitutional energy and matter exchange routes that integrate system states in space. To be sure, whenever energy and matter are exchanged, information is transmitted. But the information flow characterizing a horizon is a residue, a durable by-product of prior matter and/or energy exchanges. Like traditions, horizons express the information contained in but a few of the technologies found in a given phase. But unlike traditions the information exchange that accompanies horizons is subject to the dissipative effects of most entropy-producing events and processes. Unless they are renewed by repeated exchanges of matter and/or energy, or they are incorporated in the institutional structure of a recipient, the information flows which mark a horizon will rapidly dissipate. It is this aspect of horizons which give them their limited duration and make them an efficient tool for integrating far-flung phases in space. It is, however, those cases in which the information flows accompanying a horizon are incorporated in the institutional structure of a recipient that are most interesting. Under the proper circumstances they may create the demand for continuing exchanges of matter and energy, thus providing a durability that the horizon might not otherwise attain. We are referring here to those special cases known as the Archaic and Hopewell interaction spheres, cases in which the spread and incorporation of information seem to have conferred durability.

We may now describe variants as multiphase but not suprainstitutional system-state trajectories. Thus we may understand variants as time- and/or space-ordered sequences of system states whose component transformations individually and collectively are consistent with a single kind of equilibrium, either steady state, metastable, or dynamic (see Clarke 1968, 51). These trajectories represent the interaction of institution-channeled information, matter, and energy flows with external forces which have shaped but have not disrupted systemic integration. In other words, the dissipative effects of entropy-producing events and processes have modified the intensity of information, matter, and energy exchanges beyond that consistent with our interpretation of phase but not beyond our ability to see and understand systemic coherence.

There is a sense in which our use of *variant* resembles the prior notion of archaeological culture, and at first we were tempted to use it in this way. But the customary construal of an archaeological culture has static and atomistic connotations we wanted to avoid. Hence we prefer trajectories in time and space to trait complexes even though the former are inferred from the latter by approximating the direction inherent in just-so similarities among artifacts and artifact by-products. Then too, we wanted to keep the potential inhering in distinguishing relative stability in time from relative stability in space. Insofar as we are restricted by the evidence available to trajectories in time, variants may be construed as institution-channeled minitraditions. Insofar as the same is true for trajectories in space, variants may be considered institution-channeled minihorizons. It is only when we have the evidence to certify the co-occurrence of institution-channeled trajectories in both space and time that variants resemble archaeological cultures. We certainly should seek the requisite evidence, but until we have it we must confine ourselves to trajectories in either time or space.

Our interpretations thus far may be summarized as follows:

    Subsystem = Institution
    Component = Community
        Phase = System state (multicommunity, institution-channeled matter, energy and information exchange climax)
     Tradition = Suprainstitutional information exchange route
      Horizon = Suprainstitutional matter and energy exchange route

Variant = Institution-channeled multiphase system trajectory in time, in space, or in both time and space

We shall use phases as the classificatory taxa of greatest specificity, and traditions, variants, and horizons as the primary integrative units, that is, as those most useful for the presentation and interpretation of intra-areal relationships. Nevertheless, to be effective these units must be restricted to a given region or area. For more inclusive synthesis, other taxonomic units must be devised or adopted—units that are free from the strict temporal and spatial limitations that inhere in phases, traditions, horizons, and variants. We need, in effect, a taxon, or set of taxa, which can articulate our subregional or subareal synthesis with its panregional or panareal counterpart. In seeking such a taxon, or set of taxa, we might, at first, suppose that the differences between subregional and subareal syntheses and their regional or areal counterparts are just a matter of scale. If we adopted this view, however, we would be badly mistaken. The larger does not merely subsume the smaller but is selectively created from it. The existing area or regional syntheses are in fact highly selective. From the welter of local details, our predecessors chose only those they saw as having the greatest regional or areawide significance and emphasized them at the expense of all others (see Caldwell 1958; Lehmer 1971). Thus our problem is more complex than at first might be supposed. We must understand the elements given greatest weight in existing areal or regional syntheses; we must independently weigh the details of the local archaeological record, selecting those elements suitable for our own subregional or subareal synthesis; and we must be able to test the adequacy of the former against the latter; that is, we must use those previously proposed region or areawide taxa that are most compatible with their local counterparts if we wish to make their comparison a meaningful task. It is to this latter issue that we now turn.

Other Taxonomic Issues

In 1958 J. R. Caldwell (1958) provided a synthesis of eastern prehistory based upon the recognition of classificatory units he called trends and traditions. He construed a tradition as a "main-line areally based continuity of what would theoretically be a cultural whole" (1958, 33). He apparently wanted the term to apply to the broadest recognizable continuities in patterns of understanding and action. To quote him on this point: "In reserving tradition as a special term for whole cultural continuities, we but follow a trend from Willey's original formulation of pottery tradition (1945) through Goggin's whole cultural traditions of Florida (1949) to the base regional tradition known as Gulf (Sears 1954)" (Caldwell 1958, 3). Caldwell (1958, 3), in fact, expanded Sears's Gulf Tradition by giving it greater time depth. Caldwell's traditions in general assign greater synthetic force to persistence in time than to stability in space. As a consequence, his traditions seem anchorless. They flow like waves from place to place, here being manifested earlier, there later, but secured to no single place for the duration. These broad wavelike traditions are, in turn, composed of trends which Caldwell (1958, 3) describes as "an interplay of more localized cultural streams of shorter duration." These trends are, in effect, merely scaled-down versions of his traditions into which they are subsumed. Consider for instance the following: "These (Trends) we can define in exactly the same way as the greater traditions; in terms of maximum significant contrast. *These local traditions* which might be considered phases or foci in temporal depth more often coincide with particular ecological areas and may show detailed patterns of continuities and change from which their local histories may be inferred" (1958, 3–4; italics ours). Thus, trends are currents and eddies which flow through ecological areas as these areas are swept by the waves of one or another tradition. Finally, Caldwell (1958, 3–5) sees the waves of various traditions moving with and against one another toward climax in a kind of economic adjustment he construes as primary in the sense of fostering the most efficient use of local resources. His is an ingenious scheme and one that serves its purpose well. If we desire, as Caldwell (1958, 2) does, a contextual history—that is, a picture of "historical flow, the constant generation of events out of previous contexts, in effect, the very dynamism now to be found in the usual histories based on written records"—then we might be predisposed to use it. We might also wish to use it if we had broader, more ambitious theoretical interests. For example, the expectable consequence of Caldwell's approach, its most useful and desirable product, is a "non-nuclear" culture type which could be used in delineating those "cultural balances with which expanding civilizations are everywhere confronted" (Caldwell 1958). But this is not our goal. We have a far more limited interest and purpose.

The adequacy of Caldwell's trends and traditions is difficult, if not impossible, to evaluate using purely local materials and sequences. His traditions are too broadly conceived for our purposes. From our perspective, which perforce is a decidedly narrow and local one, Caldwell's traditions seem to be fleeting and ephemeral or stable yet ethereal. They wash over and surround rather than flow through the events and processes which shape local affairs. His trends seem, at first, to be more restricted, more substantial, more suited to our purpose. But on closer examination, two out of three of them also flow too far and too fast for our needs. The first trend, an increasing efficiency in exploiting the forest, manifested in the development of ambush hunting, seasonal cycles, and the discovery of new sources of natural foods, can be tested, albeit with difficulty, against purely local materials (Caldwell 1958, 6–17). The second, an era of regional differentiation and stylistic change, cannot (Caldwell 1958, 19–52). Nor can the third, which is a "progressive drawing together with the Nuclear American Civilization" (Caldwell 1958, 60–71). In short, when Caldwell's scheme departs from purely techno-environmental considerations, as it must, we are at a loss. We cannot evaluate it from the purely local perspective forced upon us by our data. The relative emphasis placed upon space, time, and content in Caldwell's scheme is so different as to be incompatible with subareal or subregional synthesis of the kind we propose. We must, therefore, seek an alternative.

The Willey and Phillips Stage

The most popular alternative is the system of configurational stages introduced by Willey and Phillips (1958, 61–193). These stages are derived from narrower, more explicitly described and tangibly precise traditions. Nevertheless, their formation was not a part of the "method of systematic historical integration" that produced traditions, horizons, and phases (Willey and Phillips 1958, 64–65). We thus have the precision, yet separate derivation, that we desire. As for the elements given greatest weight we can clearly anticipate that the content and form of technological-environmental interaction will be accorded special attention. Willey and Phillips (1958, 68) point with approval to Kreiger's (1953) claim that each stage should be "a segment of historical sequence in a given area characterized by a *dominating pattern of economic existence*" (italics ours). They also agree that "a stage may be recognized by content alone" (Willey and Phillips 1958, 69). It would thus be fair to say that the Willey and Phillips stage, insofar as it can be said to exist in a given area or region, consists of an integrated complex of social, political, and economic practices which collectively express a common pattern of economic adjustment. That this pattern of economic adjustment must not be ephemeral is clear enough, but beyond stipulating that it be part of a historical developmental sequence, Willey and Phillips (1958, 61–78) *make no claims about its persistence maxima or minima*. They prefer, instead, the independent formulation of time and content units. For example, they laud the formulation of stages and periods as described by Kreiger (1953, 247). The term *period* "might be considered to depend upon chronology (alone). . . . the same stage may be said to appear at different times or periods in different areas and also to end at different times." Quite clearly then, Willey and Phillips would have us independently derive stages and periods—time in this part of their formulation is to be divorced from content, that is, it is to be treated as it would be if the M.T.S. were being used. Stages, it seems, should succeed one another (in historical developmental sequence) but must be defined on content alone.

The precise construal accorded the Willey and Phillips conception of historical developmental sequence thus becomes one of great interpretive import. We should at this point examine what they have done as well as what they say they have done. Willey and Phillips (1958, 75) have organized the prehistory of the whole Western Hemisphere into the following succession of stages: Lithic, Archaic, Formative, Classic, and Post-Classic. The Mississippian manifestations discussed later in this book represent the zenith of the Formative stage (see Jennings 1974, 246). They are preceded by less populous and less complex formulations traditionally called Woodland (Griffin 1966, 117; Willey 1966, 267). They are followed by less populous, less complex Formative formulations termed Protohistoric (see Sheldon 1974). More to the point, however, is that remains attributed to the Lithic, Archaic, and Formative stages have been found in North America, but representatives of the Classic and Post-Classic stages are absent north of the Rio Grande (Willey and Phillips 1958, 183). Put in less tendentious terms, colonial Euro-Americans encountered Amerindian confederacies and small-scale chiefdoms (social forms representing the Formative stage) during their westward expansion. They did not find the states and empires (social forms representing the Classic and Post-Classic stages) that confronted the Spanish in Mexico and western South America.

Why states and empires should have flourished in Latin America but not in North America is a vexing question. That a satisfactory answer will demand recourse to the advent of agriculture and the technology and population growth that it sustained cannot be doubted (see Sanders and Price 1968). But can their relatively brief experience as cultivators account for the lack of native North American states and empires? To reframe the question, given sufficient time, would North American Indians have become state and empire builders? An affirmative answer requires an orderly march toward civilization. It implies that all Amerindian societies were responding to the beat of the same drummer. Some were just a bit slower than the rest. A negative answer calls into question the end toward which all Amerindian societies were moving. It implies, as Caldwell (1958, vi) put it, that "civilization might indeed be something rather special, possibly abnormal, as it certainly can be an uncomfortable, condition of cultural development."

To sharpen the focus yet further let us ask, do the Mississippian manifestations in the Tombigbee, and by extension those in the rest of Alabama, prefigure the emergence of states and empires? If so, then the protohistoric organizational simplification (see Sheldon 1974) and population decline was but an interlude, a pause, a brief hiatus in the gathering of momentum. States and empires would have been inevitable if Euro-American conquest had not intervened. If not, then the Mississippian manifestations we shall later discuss represented a culture climax, a pinnacle of momentum gathered, an example of the ultimate in the expressed potential of a social, economic, and political structuring which in and of itself could have gone no further. From the latter perspective, the protohistoric simplification of social, political, and economic life was more than an interlude. It was instead a waning of momentum, a dissipation of organizational force, which in the absence of additional and external pressures could not have been reformulated to the end of state and empire building.

We thus have a potential conflict of perspective inhering in the construal of stages as "historical developmental" units. As might be expected, this potential has expressed itself in the work of our colleagues. There are those so firmly committed to the inevitability of state and empire formation that they describe at least some Mississippian manifestations as states, although the evidence for this interpretation is unconvincing (see Gibbon 1974). Others, no less sanguine in their view, argue that native American achievements, the Mississippian enterprise among them, exemplify a pattern of development which, in and of itself, would never have led to statehood (Caldwell 1958). They interpret the available data as evidence for a pattern of development which is "non-nuclear."

Toward an Interpretation of Stage

The consequences of a non-nuclear pattern of development need further attention. In a sense, all social development prior to the advent of food production can be construed as non-nuclear. The authors of the stage concept we are considering implicitly recognize this fact: "The criteria for dividing pre-agricultural stages are essentially technological. They refer to artifact types and traditions in technology. The criteria for dividing stages above the threshold of agriculture take reference in much more complex data. They pertain to social and political organization, religion, aesthetics—to the whole of what Redfield has termed the 'moral order' " (Willey and Phillips 1958, 72–73). That the "moral order" is necessarily more complex than the technological order is a debatable point. Nevertheless, it is strikingly clear that Willey and Phillips consider the separation of hunting and gathering from food production to be of considerable importance. In their own words:

It should be recognized that no other differentiation between stages with which we will deal has the same profundity and significance as this one. In this we are in agreement with Robert Braidwood and Robert Redfield who see the old world "urban revolution," or "dawn of civilization" as something that was

made possible by the establishment of agriculture several millenniums earlier,
but not as marking a technological and economic shift as profound as the one
from food-gathering to food production. [Willey and Phillips 1958, 72]

But does the advent of food production necessarily set those people who in-
vent or accept it upon the path to civilization? Could it not be the case that
food production in non-nuclear regions might lead to a kind of social, political, economic, and demographic stasis which resists rather than promotes the
formation of those social forms characteristic of the state? Thus in native
North America may the Formative not be part of a historical developmental
sequence which was leading to different ends? We think that we can build an
arguably productive case for this point and will therefore suggest that for
North America the Willey and Phillips stage requires a reworking to rid it of
some of the nuances it has come to contain. Since a knowledge of these
nuances must be derived from the patterning presumed to inhere in the North
American archaeological record, it might be well to examine the record,
avoiding for the moment the eastern woodlands but contrasting North America's other non-nuclear regions with the nuclear region of Mesoamerica.

By 15,000 years ago hunting and gathering peoples had spread through
western North America, Mexico, and perhaps beyond (MacNeish 1971, 36–
46; Willey 1971). Their southward spread reached Tierra del Fuego at the
southern tip of South America by 10,000 years ago (MacNeish 1971, 36–46).
Their spread eastward to the Atlantic seaboard seems to have been equally
rapid (Willey 1966). Hence by 8000 B.C., perhaps a bit earlier, the Western
Hemisphere was settled by hunting and harvesting peoples whose lifestyle
seems remarkably homogeneous (Wormington, in press). This homogeneity,
which may be more apparent than real, does, nonetheless, allow us to use the
Great Plains of North America as a kind of test section for anticipating the
patterning of social development expected of early hunting groups farther
south and east.

In the Great Plains of North America, two distinct forms of fluted projectile
points, one found exclusively with mammoth, the other with extinct bison and
the stratigraphic superposition of the two, established a sequence of early
mammoth hunters and later bison hunters (Cotter 1937, 1–16; Sellards 1952,
29–31; Wormington 1957, 47–51). The food requirements of mammoths presumably exceed the potential of the short steppe grasses that now dominate the
region, hence a more luxuriant past plant cover must be posited (Wedel 1961,
58–59). The general picture that has emerged from research on this element of
an early human ecology is one of a cooler, moister climate which supported a
lush prairie grassland. Many of the mammoth kills in this region were, in fact,
found in or near ancient ponds, streams, or river channels. Further, a significant proportion of the beasts slaughtered at these locales were female, young,

or immature. This evidence led some to infer selectivity on the part of the hunters and to posit a pattern of single elephant kills at favored hunting stations (Haury 1953; Wedel 1961, 59). With the disappearance of the elephant (for reasons not yet satisfactorily explained) hunting and gathering peoples turned to the smaller but more abundant grazing animals, chief among them a bison of larger than modern size (Skinner and Kaiser 1947, 171). Mass kills resembling drives, or pounds, and opportunistic surrounds or ambushes at water holes or in the breaks along water courses or drainage ways replaced the earlier pattern of repetitious single animal kills (Wedel 1961, 60–65). This shift from single large animal kills to the mass slaughter of smaller animals or taking of solitary forms may be far more important than we now assume. It could, for instance, have forced the emergence of those basic principles of personal management and conflict resolution upon which larger and more stable population aggregates were ultimately built. At any rate, it was from the protean base provided by early hunters and harvesters whether in Mexico, the Great Plains, or elsewhere, that the events of succeeding millennia shaped a rich diversity of lifestyles.

For the next 6,000 years the multiplex web of human, animal, and plant relationships expanded and intensified as the economies of hunting and gathering groups responded to the food potentials of different regions. The early post-Pleistocene food potentials of Mexico, the southwestern United States, the Great Plains of North America, and perhaps of the Southeast were set, in part, by the altithermal, a period characterized by higher temperatures and lower rainfall than is typical today (Antevs 1955, Deevey and Flint 1957, Flint 1947, Quimby 1954). In Mexico and the American Southwest, lush well-watered plains were slowly replaced by arid lands with a xyrophilic plant cover (Coe 1962, 43–45). To the north in the Great Plains, short grass communities expanded into areas occupied by tall grasses, parts of the modern short grass plains (e.g., the Bighorn and Wyoming basins) possessed a Great Basin type ecology, and stands of oak-hickory forest along upland tributaries were reduced or eliminated (Reeves 1973, 1227; Wedel 1978, 196). There is intriguing evidence for episodic shifts from forest edge to prairie biotypes in the Ozarks (Wood and McMillan 1976). The effects of the altithermal, if any, have yet to be adequately measured farther east, but there may have been an eastward spread of grasslands to portions of the southeastern United States (T. Lewis, 1954, 11–13).

The effects of the altithermal were being felt in Mexico as early as 7000 B.C. The course of subsequent events there is exemplified by the pattern of development in the Tehuacán valley south of Mexico City. Here, dessication led to a gradual redistribution of plants and animals, which ultimately concentrated them about available water sources. The human inhabitants responded by adjusting their hunting tools and techniques, extending and intensifying their collecting practices, and equipping themselves with more efficient tools and implements for the preparation of plant foods. The better-watered regions now served as focal areas, pockets of periodic but intense interaction between man and plants (Flannery 1968a).

Men still subsisted as hunters and harvesters, but as millennium followed millennium, the focalization of human and plant behavior led first to plant tending, then to full-scale cultivation. Full-scale cultivation, and perhaps some of the forms of plant tending which preceded it, forced incremental increases in residential stability such that by 3000 B.C. clusters of timber, grass, and dirt-covered pit houses were to be found near the better-watered strips of tillable land (see MacNeish 1964a, 1964b, 1967). These earthlodge clusters are good presumptive evidence for the emergence of a mixed hunting, collecting, and farming economy adjusted to a seasonal cycle, featuring periods of village life interspersed with periods of hunting and gathering. The first faltering steps toward full-scale farming and year-round village life had been taken. In Mexico, once this threshold had been passed, there was no turning back—the economic import of farming continued to grow at the expense of hunting and gathering.

By 1000 B.C. Mexico was occupied by village-dwelling farming folk (Coe 1966, 42; Hammond 1977). The prevailing pattern of settlement was one of small, autonomous farming communities each dependent upon locally available resources. The inhabitants of such communities presumably had equal access to the means of production, and the exploitative tasks performed in any one community were similar in type and scheduling to the tasks performed in every other. At any rate, the tools and strategies used for procuring and processing locally available raw materials seem to have been similar for most groups. Under such conditions, seasonal differences in intergroup surpluses must have been minimal, any trade in foodstuffs, raw materials, or indigenous manufactured goods restricted, and the economic incentives for supracommunity management of social and natural resources limited. Yet the foundations of a kinship-based internally ranked authority structure must have been laid in these early communities. The earliest suprahousehold forms of authority were probably a response to the need for conflict resolution and the need to organize and schedule community labor. Whatever the case may have been, early authority structures seem to have been weakly developed and purely local. The overall picture is one of a sparse populace gathered together in small communities, each independent of the comings and goings of others, each, in effect, a nation unto itself (Coe 1966, 42–46). An important transition had, however, been fully realized. Food was now moved to and among people. Upon this foundation a new and stratified, as opposed to ranked, social order was raised.

Mexico's regionally distinct village farming traditions formed the weft threads in the emergent tapestry of state and empire. The warps were provided by commerce and conquest. Both were driven, in slightly different ways, by the shuttle of population growth. But in more prosaic terms, we may see two pathways, or routes, to state and empirehood; one through conquest, which emerged in environmentally circumscribed areas; the other through the pull of market centers in areas with an uneven distribution of important natural resources.

State formation through conquest requires an initial phase in which population growth produces demographic stress which may be temporarily relieved by the reorganization of labor and technology to the end of irrigation, terracing, or reclamation of swamps and other marginal lands. If, however, population continues to grow with no relief via emigration, then demographic stress will again assert its influence by promoting competition for available resources and inciting conquest warfare. Conquest warfare, with its incorporation of vanquished by victor, will lead, we presume, to multicommunity forms of economic integration and will produce the administrative apparatus needed to direct and control newly acquired human and natural resources (Carneiro 1970, 733–38).

For state formation via the market, we must assume that a multicommunity exchange net, in an area characterized by the uneven distribution of resources, became focused upon a strategically located settlement and converted it to a trade center. Further, we must assume that this trade center attracted and at least partially supported, religious functionaries, artisans, craftsmen, merchants, and other specialists or quasi specialists whose presence augmented the local population and added to the natural growth rate of the community. We must also contend that during this process some of the community's specialists or quasi specialists (most probably those with combined civil and religious responsibility) acquired power and prestige by virtue of liens against the goods and services channeled through the market such that they formed the administrative nucleus needed to organize and direct conquest warfare if that became necessary. Thus when the local populace swelled to the demographic stress point and the demands for an inflow of goods exceeded the supply available, the center had both the organizational structure and the manpower to extend its demands upon the productive power of the hinterland either by (1) economic threat and intimidation or (2) military venture. Population densities in the hinterland may have remained low, and a pattern of fight and flight may have still obtained there unless or until formerly autonomous communities were incorporated into the net of control cast by the market center (Flannery 1968b, Rathje 1971, Sanders 1968).

In Mexico, these two patterns of growth were not mutually exclusive. Singularly or jointly, by 800 b.c., they stimulated the formation of states. The Olmec civilization of Vera Cruz and Tabasco was a good example (Drucker, Heizer, and Squier 1959; Stirling 1940). The Monte Alban formulation in Oaxaca was another. The valley of Mexico spawned the equally early market

center of Tlaltilco (Pina Chan 1958) and by the first century A.D. had become
the home of the greatest of all pre-Columbian Mexican commercial centers,
Teotihuacán (Coe 1962, Linné 1934, Wolf 1959). Teotihuacán was a true city,
an unequivocal example of urbanism, which at its height contained 20 square
kilometers of temples, plazas, workshops, palaces, apartments, slums,
drainage systems, waterways, and reservoirs organized about a grid system of
avenues and streets (Millon 1970). Teotihuacán was also the center of a vast
commercial empire that serviced populations in Vera Cruz, Tabasco, Oaxaca,
and the Mayan regions of Mexico and Guatemala (Coe 1962, 115).

North of Mexico and west of the Mississippi River, the postaltithermal
rhythm to event and process was different. Along the Pacific Coast the abundant plant and animal life permitted a truly remarkable fine-tuning of postaltithermal hunting and harvesting economies. Once a workable balance had
been achieved here it proved extremely durable. There were, to be sure, periodic economic adjustments as a consequence of human initiative or variations
in the behavior of plants and animals, but they never exceeded the limits of a
dynamic equilibrium as realized within the confines of a hunting and harvesting lifestyle (see Hester and Grady 1982, 357–62). Across the coastal
mountains in the arid and semiarid basins and plateaus to the east, a desert
culture, reminiscent of the earliest postaltithermal adjustments in Mexico, led
to sparse and mobile populations which, once integrated with a scarce resource base, proved equally resistant to change. The desert culture achieved in
this region persisted virtually unaltered into historic times (Steward 1938; D.
Thomas 1973, 155–76).

In the American Southwest, particularly in those regions suitable for dry
land farming and small-scale irrigation agriculture, a desert culture lifestyle
gave way to a mixed farming and hunting economy. Here and there clusters of
timber, grass, and dirt-covered pit houses, some lined with stone slabs, were
to be found near the better-watered stretches of tillable land. Like their counterparts in the Tehuacán valley, these earthlodge settlements indicate a seasonal cycle featuring periods of village life interspersed with intervals of hunting
and gathering. In subsequent millennia semisedentary village life lapsed into
either (1) full-scale village farming centered upon blocks of adjacent masonry
rooms or (2) large-scale irrigation agriculture which supported sizable villages
of above-ground timber, grass, and earth-covered houses. Isolated masonry
room blocks gave way to the multistoried, multiroomed pueblo towns of the
fourteenth, fifteenth, and sixteenth centuries. Similar towns and the lifestyle
they exemplified persisted into historic times. Large-scale irrigation agriculture and the sizable earthlodge villages it once supported collapsed by the
fifteenth century A.D. (see Kidder 1968).

A seriously reduced carrying capacity during the altithermal seems to have
forced the inhabitants of the Great Plains into oasis areas or peripheral re-

gions, where they developed a diversified lifestyle (Wedel 1964, 200). It was from this diversified lifestyle that the postaltithermal differences in fauna and flora shaped a mosaic of adjustments. Among the elements of this mosaic were (1) a highly mobile pattern of herd animal hunting and high plains foraging in the western short grass plains, (2) a less mobile, mixed woodland and tall grass plains form of hunting and harvesting along the network of creek and river courses in the central plains, and (3) a yet more sedentary woodland-adapted pattern of hunting and gathering focused upon the broad-forested bottomlands of the major river valleys and feeder streams which edged the plains on the east (see Wedel 1961, 88–94).

A mixed hunting and farming lifestyle characterized by hamlets and homesteads composed of square earthlodges; the cultivation of maize, beans, sunflowers, and tobacco; and the hunting of buffalo, deer, antelope, and smaller, more solitary, game animals appeared in the central and eastern portions of the plains by A.D. 800. Larger farming villages, composed of long, rectangular earth-covered houses surrounded by dry moats and bastioned palisades, appeared about the same time but were confined to the trough of the Missouri River and immediate environs in northern Iowa and southern South Dakota (see Wedel 1961, 164–209).

The next millennium was marked by shifts in population density and distribution. There was, for example, (1) an abandonment of the western reaches of settlement, (2) an intensification of population scattering farther to the east, (3) the emergence of large farming villages composed of circular earthlodges along the northern and eastern margins of the plains, and (4) the extension of maize agriculture and village farming to its limit in northern North Dakota. Nevertheless, the village level of sociocultural integration was never superseded. Nor were multicommunity aggregates of any size or permanence formed (see Lehmer 1970, 1971).

The foregoing exposition indicates, to us at least, that stages need not succeed one another in an inexorable sequence. While it is true that the Lithic stage everywhere precedes the Archaic, the Archaic does not everywhere precede the Formative, and the Formative does not everywhere precede the Classic, or the Classic, the Post-Classic. Only in the nuclear regions are all stages represented, and only in the nuclear regions do they all occur in a strict serial order. Then too, there seem to be real developmental differences between nuclear and non-nuclear areas. In the nuclear areas we have evidence for a massive interference with the natural environment; in non-nuclear regions we have a history of successive adjustments to it. In the nuclear areas we have evidence for large-scale long-distance trade in sufficient volume to support craft specialization and encourage bureaucratic manipulation of supply and demand. Elsewhere we have intertribal exchanges and small-scale trading expeditions which at best supported part-time craft specialization and a pattern of authority based upon redistribution. In the nuclear areas we have evidence of wars of conquest and territorial acquisition; elsewhere a pattern of raid and counterraid or blood feud obtained.

Are these apparent differences real, or is the non-nuclear sequence merely incomplete? Must we assume that the order found in nuclear areas should assert itself in non-nuclear areas as well, or have we perhaps let our commitment to a particular interpretation of the expression "historical developmental sequence" predispose us to accept an unacceptable answer? Differently phrased, must stages, as it has been commonly assumed, occur only in series? Our answer is no. We think stages can be independently defined for nuclear and non-nuclear regions. In fact, we think they must be because the processes that shaped historical development in these areas were themselves different. To hold this position with systematic rigor, however, will require that historical developmental sequences customarily construed as series be interpreted instead as quasi-serial orders.

Formal Considerations in Framing Stages

If a sequence of stages is to be a series, each stage within it must occur at one and only one position. In a series, the Formative stage and only the Formative stage may occur after the Archaic and before the Classic. In a quasi series, several different stages may occupy a given position, but as we shall see later, only in different areas or regions. Thus, if stages are to be parts of a quasi series, a Woodland stage may occur after the Archaic and before the Mississippian stage in one region, while a new stage, the Gulf Formational, for instance, might be inserted between the Archaic and Woodland stages in another. At first glance, the change from series to quasi series carries with it the potential for unencumbered stage creation—a potential which could lead to taxonomic chaos. In fact, the step from stages as strict series to stages as quasi-serial orders has already been taken in North America. It was accomplished by North Americans when they separated the Archaic from the Formative by interposing an intermediate "Woodland" hunting and gathering stage (Griffin 1966, 117; Willey 1966, 267). Further, the North American Formative has become synonymous with Mississippian, the latter having been given a rather loose construal to make it a suitable synonym (Willey and Phillips 1958, 163–70). Taxonomic chaos has not been induced by these changes, and we presume it will not be if the criteria for an appropriate quasi series are met when new taxa are proposed. That is to say, each proposed member of an acceptable quasi series must meet fairly rigorous conditions of content suitability, precedence, and coincidence.

We have already discussed the content conditions that stages are expected to express. The conditions of coincidence and precedence that each phase, tradition, horizon, and/or variant within a stage and the stage itself must meet can be stated as follows. Let x, y, and z represent either phases, traditions, horizons, and/or variants; or let them represent stages themselves. Let (C) indicate coincidence and (P) precedence. Coincidence, (C), will be considered transitive whenever x stands in (C) to y and y stands in (C) to z such that x stands in (C) to z. Coincidence will be considered reflexive whenever x stands in (C) to itself. Precedence will be considered transitive whenever x stands in (P) to y and y stands in (P) to z such that x stands in (P) to z. Precedence will be considered (C)-connected whenever x does not stand in (C) to y such that x stands in (P) to y or y stands in (P) to x. We may now define the members of a stage as those phases, traditions, horizons, and variants which exemplify the same fundamental economic adjustment, and in which coincidence is transitive, symmetric, and reflexive, and precedence is transitive, coincidence irreflexive, and coincidence connected. We may define a stage itself as that part of a regional or areal developmental sequence which exhibits relative uniformity in content and in which coincidence is reflexive and precedence is transitive and coincidence is connected. With our taxonomic preferences, biases, assumptions, and predilections as a background, let us proceed to a synthesis of the archaeological materials from the Tombigbee Waterway. We will render an interpretation of the region's archaeological sequence in the concluding section of the book.

2. The Gulf Formational Stage

The best-documented early archaeological complexes in the Tombigbee drainage belong to the Gulf Formational stage proposed by Walthall and Jenkins (1976). This stage is the third in a five-stage quasi series. This quasi series, which to our knowledge is not replicated elsewhere, is centered on the coastal plain. The stages within the quasi series are, from earliest to latest: Lithic (Paleo-Indian), Archaic, Gulf Formational, Woodland, and Mississippian (Jenkins 1982, Walthall 1980). In basic economic adjustment the Gulf Formational is no different from its Archaic predecessor. But in content, all Gulf Formational phases, traditions, horizons, and variants can be clearly and consistently segregated from their Archaic predecessors because they contain ceramics (Walthall and Jenkins 1976). Gulf Formational complexes can also be clearly separated from their Woodland successors by virtue of significant differences in economic adjustment, ceramic manufacturing practices, population size and distribution, and ceremonial and burial customs (Walthall 1980).

Traditions

The appearance and exclusive use of "Gulf tradition ceramics" marked the beginning of the Gulf Formational stage at different times in different areas of the coastal plain (Caldwell 1958). The earliest Gulf tradition ceramics were mass modeled and fiber tempered—later Gulf tradition wares were coiled and sand tempered. The Gulf tradition was characterized by incised, punctated, pinched, and/or shell-stamped (including rocker and dentate forms) designs applied to globular or flat-bottomed cylindrical vessels with podal supports or annular base appendages (Walthall and Jenkins 1976, 48). The frequent occurrence of flat bases and the occasional use of nodes punched through from the vessel interior (bosses) just below the lip were also characteristic. Griffin (1946, 49) has observed that some of these characteristics are to be found here and there in northern ceramics, but as a group they characterize southern coastal plain ceramics prior to 500 B.C. The appearance and ultimate dominance of northern, middle eastern, and southern Appalachian ceramic traditions (see Caldwell 1958), here earlier, there later, signal the end of the Gulf Formational and onset of the Woodland stage in the coastal plain.

Periods

The Gulf Formational stage may be divided into Early (2500 to 1000 B.C.), Middle (1000 to 500 B.C.) and Late (500 to 100 B.C.) periods (Jenkins 1982, 50). In the Early Gulf Formational period, ceramic manufacture was confined to the eastern coastal plain where it was represented by the fiber-tempered mass-modeled pottery of the Stallings Island and Orange series (Bullen 1972, Fairbanks 1942, Stoltman 1972). In the Middle Gulf Formational period the manufacture of mass-modeled, fiber-tempered ceramics spread to the western coastal plain, where it was represented by the Wheeler series (Wimberly 1960). In the Middle period, the manufacture of Wheeler series pottery was found in the central and upper Tombigbee drainage (Haag 1942, Jenkins 1975b). Three major events mark the Late Gulf Formational period: fiber-tempered pottery was no longer made, the manufacture of Tchefuncte and Alexander series ceramics spread through the western coastal plain, and paddle-stamped Early Woodland pottery of the Deptford type first appeared in the eastern coastal plain (Jenkins 1982, 60).

Variants

The western part of the southern coastal plain hosted three spatial variants during the Middle period of the Gulf Formational stage. The eastern and southernmost of these, the Bayou La Batre variant, was centered upon Mobile, Baldwin, and Clarke counties (fig. 4) in southern Alabama (Wimberly 1960). Bayou La Batre variant potters were the first in the Alabama region to manufacture a coiled, grit-tempered ware (Trickey 1971). Two vessel shapes, a flaring side beaker and a globular pot, predominated. Both might have either annular bases or mammiform feet. Of these vessels, 20 to 30 percent carried rocker-stamped designs (fig. 5). Bone tools included deer-bone

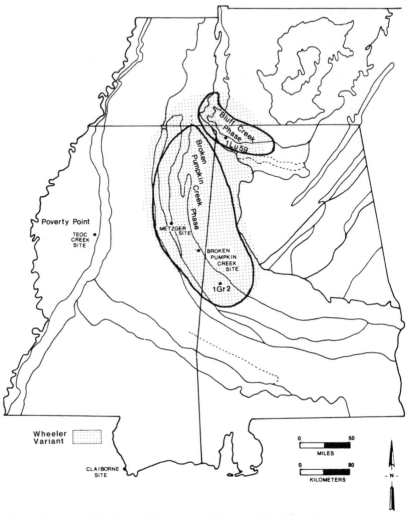

Figure 4. Selected Middle Gulf Formational Sites and Manifestations

awls, antler punches, gouges, and barbed fish hooks. Lithic tools, most made of Tallahatta quartzite, included bifaces, blades, knives, scrapers, gravers, and projectile points (Chase 1972). The projectile points were predominantly late archaic types like Pickwick, Little Bear Creek, and Ledbetter (fig. 5). The distribution and content of known Bayou La Batre variant sites suggest a pattern of interior forest hunting and harvesting and coastal foraging on the part of a population in steady state (i.e., stable) equilibrium with its natural resources (see Walthall 1980, 95–98).

The Poverty Point variant was centered on the lower Mississippi valley to the north and west of Bayou La Batre territory (Ford and Webb 1956). Poverty Point populations show that kind of vigor which accompanies a dynamic equilibrium between population and environment. The construction of earthworks, some of considerable size and complexity; the spread of ceramics (fig. 5), including solid clay figurines and other baked clay objects of Poverty Point authorship; and the manufacture of microblade perforators, end scrapers, side scrapers and needles, perforated and unperforated beads, and pendants attest to the creation and manipulation of wealth, a portion of which may be attributed to trade. The Poverty Point site, for instance, was strategically located near the confluence of six major rivers, an optimal position for control of the riverine trade routes which presumably formed the major threads of a rather extensive trade net (Walthall 1980, 85–87). The movement of galena from the Great Lakes, steatite from the Piedmont, orthoquartzite or Tallahatta quartzite from southern Alabama, novaculite and crystal quartz from Arkansas, Stallings Island pottery from either the Chattahoochee drainage or the Atlantic Coast, and Saint Johns pottery from Florida to and through Poverty Point and other Poverty Point variant sites like Claiborne indicates the important role played by trade (Brasher 1973; Gibson 1973, 1974, 1979; Webb 1977; Winters 1968). In fact, pottery of the Wheeler series, the earliest in Mississippi and Alabama, was probably a by-product of the trade funneled through and managed by Poverty Point variant peoples (Jenkins 1982, 60).

Although the Wheeler variant was centered upon the western Tennessee valley (fig. 4), outliers could be found throughout eastern Mississippi and western Alabama (Jenkins 1982, 54–58). Wheeler variant potters manufactured coiled, fiber-tempered, flat-bottomed, widemouthed beakers and simple flat-bottomed bowls with outsloping sides. Most Wheeler vessels were plain. Those pieces which were decorated carried punctate, dentate, or simple stamped designs (fig. 5). Stone tools were usually made of Fort Payne chert or Tallahatta quartzite; projectile points were of Wade, Cotaco Creek, or Motley type. The content, size, and overall distribution of Wheeler variant sites suggest a subsistence regimen geared to exploit the seasonal contrasts between forest and prairie biorhythms. Upland prairie, slope forest, and riverine hunting and harvesting patterns were integrated into an annual subsistence cycle

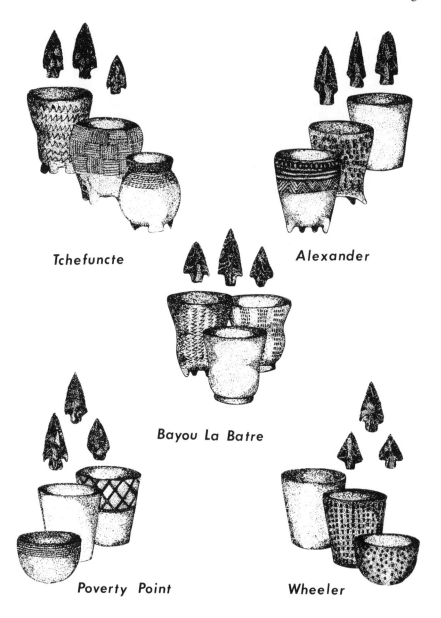

Figure 5. Artifacts of the Western Gulf Formational Variants

by the periodic abundance of deer, smaller game animals, and nut foods in each place (Jenkins 1982, 50–55). The overall picture was one of a slowly growing, infrequently declining, well-adjusted population with a fine-tuned forest edge/riverine hunting and harvesting economy in a subtle yet dynamic equilibrium with its environment; that is, peaks and troughs in its dynamism were shallow and far apart, suggesting that the integration of population with natural resources was approaching a stable equilibrium.

In the late period of the Gulf Formational stage, the Alexander variant succeeded its earlier Wheeler counterpart in the western and middle Tennessee valley; the Pickwick, Wheeler, and Guntersville basins; and in the central and upper Tombigbee drainage of Mississippi and Alabama (fig. 4) (Jenkins 1982, 60–66). Alexander variant ceramicists produced globular vessels with tetrapodal supports or annular bases, widemouthed cylindrical vessels, and flat-bottomed bowls with outsloping sides. Alexander vessels were decorated with rim bosses, incising, zoning, punctating, pinching, and to a lesser degree with rocker and dentate rocker stamping (fig. 5). The globular vessel body with tetrapodal or annular basal appendages was new to the region, as were bosses, pinching, incising, and zoning. The ideas which stimulated these manufacturing and decorating practices may have been spread to and through the Alexander variant by trade. Local interpretations and innovations were, however, responsible for the distinctive configuration of decorative and manufacturing elements that became the Alexander ceramic series. Projectile points of Flint Creek type were added to a lithic inventory which included the same range of knives, scrapers, and projectile points manufactured by Wheeler variant flintsmiths. That there was continuity between Alexander variant economic practices and those of the preceding Wheeler variant populations cannot be doubted (see Walthall 1980, 98–103). In general content and distribution of sites of different sizes, the Wheeler and Alexander variants were homologues. The forest edge/riverine hunting and harvesting economy, which in the Wheeler variant was in dynamic equilibrium with the environment, had by Alexander variant times reached a stable equilibrium which could not, without an external assist, regain its dynamism. When faced with absorption or displacement, the Alexander variant lifestyle failed to maintain its integrity.

Our processual interpretive classification has thus far allowed us to sketch only the broader patterning to be found in the western reaches of Gulf Formational territory. We have, however, created a stage internal taxonomic structure composed of variants united one with another by the Gulf tradition. The Gulf tradition flows through these variants and creates an equilibrium basin which gives direction to the various equilibrium states they express. The Gulf tradition, nevertheless, unfolds through time and integrates best when it is construed as a primarily temporal continuity to manufacturing practices—that is, as the persistence of competence in a particular technology or related cluster of technologies. We feel satisfied with the integration of our variants in time. The same is not the case for their integration in space. This task should properly be accomplished by a horizon which, remember, we will interpret as an "interphase information exchange route, or channel." Just such a "channel" for the spread of information was created, we think, by a far-flung trade in steatite.

Horizon

We view the trade in steatite as a horizon which, in the West, integrated phases of the Bayou La Batre, Wheeler, and Poverty Point variants and also integrated them with their eastern counterparts in Georgia, South Carolina, and Florida. The geological occurrence of steatite is confined to the Piedmont region. Steatite sherds and vessels are nevertheless found throughout the coastal plain from the St. Johns River area to as far west as Poverty Point. Work by Bullen and Bullen (1961) indicates an active trade by Orange Three times. At the Summer Haven site, a zone yielding Orange Three ceramics and steatite sherds was dated at 1380±200 B.C. Gagliano and Webb (1970) report a cache of steatite vessels at the Claiborne site near the mouth of the Pearl River. Claiborne also produced Stallings Island (early Wheeler) and St. Johns ceramics, numerous exotic lithics, and a wide range of Poverty Point clay balls. Such a wide variety of nonlocal materials (Gagliano and Webb 1970, table 3) leads the excavators to speculate that Claiborne and the slightly earlier Cedarland site were trading stations.

> It appears, therefore, that occupants of the Cedarland and Claiborne villages were participating in a widespread trade network, up the Mississippi valley and along the Gulf coast, which seems to have intensified in Poverty Point times. There are evidences of direct contact between the Claiborne and Poverty Point sites; it seems probable that Claiborne was a regional center of importance in the commercial, secular and religious organization of the Poverty Point cultural complex. [Gagliano and Webb 1970, 72]

Another cache of steatite vessels was found in a field adjacent to the Poverty Point site (Webb 1944). The vessel shapes, flat-bottomed beakers, were identical to those from the Claiborne site and to Wheeler and St. Johns vessel forms. Further, several of the vessel lips were diagonally engraved with simple rectilinear designs also like those at the Claiborne site. In addition, these designs are similar to those found on Orange Four ceramics and Stallings Island bone pins, where flattened lips bearing rectilinear incised decoration are documented during late Orange times (Griffin and Smith 1954, 43). One steatite vessel fragment from Poverty Point depicted a bird with outstretched wings reminiscent of the motif that later became popular as the "Hopewell raptorial bird." Steatite in the form of whole vessels or vessel fragments has also been found at nine Poverty Point sites in Louisiana, eleven sites in Mississippi, and three in Arkansas (Webb 1977, 36). Neutron activation analysis indicates that the steatite samples from these sites, with one exception, came from quarries in Georgia or eastern Alabama (Smith 1981, 120–25). It is tempting, therefore, to suggest that the Chattahoochee River served as a convenient trade artery for the movement of steatite and perhaps other items. Many of the Chattahoochee's tributaries drain the Alabama and Georgia piedmont where steatite outcrops are located. Once quarried, the steatite and other trade goods could be moved down these streams to the coast, thence by boat eastward or westward.

We have completed our regional and areal taxonomic edifice. To summarize the results: (1) we have explicated the Gulf Formational stage; (2) we have divided the Gulf Formational into three sequential periods, Early (2500 to 1000 B.C.), Middle (1000 to 500 B.C.) and Late (500 to 100 B.C.); (3) we have formed four variants, namely, Bayou La Batre (probably starts no earlier than 600–800 B.C.), Poverty Point, Wheeler, and Alexander, each of which expressed different equilibrium states; and (4) we have integrated all four of these variants in time via the Gulf tradition and three of them in space via the steatite trade which joined roughly contemporary western variants one with another and with their eastern analogues. We must now turn our attention to the subregional and subareal taxonomic structure whose basic taxon is the phase.

The Broken Pumpkin Creek Phase

Material Culture

The earliest Gulf Formational manifestation in the Tombigbee drainage was the Broken Pumpkin Creek phase of the Wheeler variant. Components of this phase were found in the central and upper Tombigbee drainage and in that portion of the lower Warrior drainage adjacent to the central Tombigbee (fig. 4) (Jenkins 1982, 54–55). The diagnostic ceramics of the Broken Pumpkin Creek phase are fiber-tempered wares of the Wheeler series, specifically Wheeler Plain, Wheeler Dentate Stamped, Wheeler Punctated, and Wheeler Simple Stamped (fig. 6) (Sears and Griffin 1950). Eighty-five to ninety percent of the Broken Pumpkin Creek pottery was plain; punctate and dentate stamped were the most frequent minority treatments. A simple stamped surface treat-

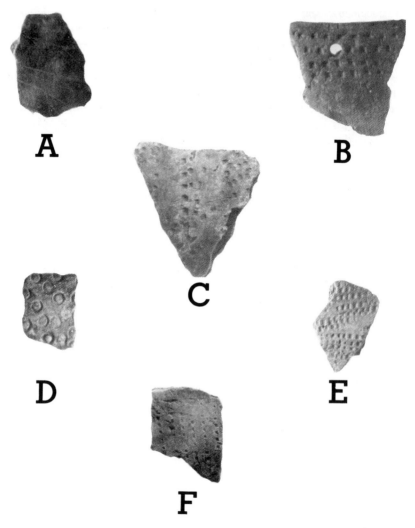

Figure 6. Pottery of the Broken Pumpkin Creek Phase: (A) Wheeler Simple Stamped; (B, D) Wheeler Punctated; (C, E, F) Wheeler Dentate Stamped

ment occurred but was relatively rare. The dominant vessel shape was a flat-bottomed beaker with a wide mouth (i.e., with outsloping sides). A simple flat-bottomed bowl with outsloping sides was a less frequent form. One restorable beaker of this kind was found at 1Gr2 (Jenkins 1972). The projectile point types associated with fiber-tempered pottery in Broken Pumpkin Creek components include those of the Wade cluster; Wade var. *Wade*, Cotaco Creek var. *Cotaco Creek,* and Motley var. *unspecified* (see Ensor 1981; Faulkner and Graham 1966; Faulkner and McCollough 1974, 320; Morse and Polhemus n.d.[b]). In projectile point manufacture in particular, and lithic technology in general, the Broken Pumpkin Creek phase exhibited continuities with its Archaic predecessors. This continuity is best shown by the persistence and predominance of local non-heat-treated stone as the major raw material and imported stone from the south as a minor raw material source (Ensor 1980, 87). Little subsistence data are available, but what we have indicate a diet of nut foods and deer meat (Caddell 1981a; Woodrick 1981).

Subsistence Practices

All nine Broken Pumpkin Creek components in the Gainesville Lake area (i.e., the middle Tombigbee) were small ephemeral campsites in the slope forests which lie between the floodplain woodlands on the upper terrace and the upland prairies (Jenkins, Curren, and DeLeon 1975). Considerably larger and presumably more prominent campsites, like the Broken Pumpkin Creek site itself, were located in the prairie or at the upland forest / prairie edge (fig. 7). All three contexts—that is, prairie, slope forest, and riverbottom woodlands—need further attention. The prairie was essentially treeless at the time of European exploration, although single trees or small clusters of oaks could be found here and there (Caddell 1981a, 16). Although the alkaline Sumter and Huston clays could support only grasslands, with few or no trees, there were portions of the prehistoric prairie in which acid Vaiden, Eutaw, and Oktibbeah soils probably supported oak forests (Swenson et al. 1941, 79A). Thus it might be better to describe the prehistoric prairie as parkland composed of an open oak forest—a context with a large amount of edge environment containing acorn mast and herbaceous undergrowth, both of which at different times of the year would have attracted sizable deer populations. Oaks also comprised the majority of trees (61 percent) in the slope forests, where they were interspersed with hickory (approximately 14 percent), walnut, beechnut, and non-nut-producing broadleafs (Caddell 1981a, 16). Hickory, oak, walnut, and beech were also found in the wooded floodplains, juxtaposed to ready sources of fish, waterfowl, and shellfish.

The distribution and harvest patterns of natural resources suggest a seasonal round in which the parklands served as a spring and summer residence and the slope forests as a fall and winter abode. In the spring and early summer, when the herbaceous undergrowth which edged the meadowlands was tender and juicy, deer would have been attracted by the prospects of easy and rich browse. Until the acorn masts of the slope forests became available in mid to late fall (i.e., October and November), deer would continue to be attracted to these edge areas, particularly in the early evening at or shortly before dusk.

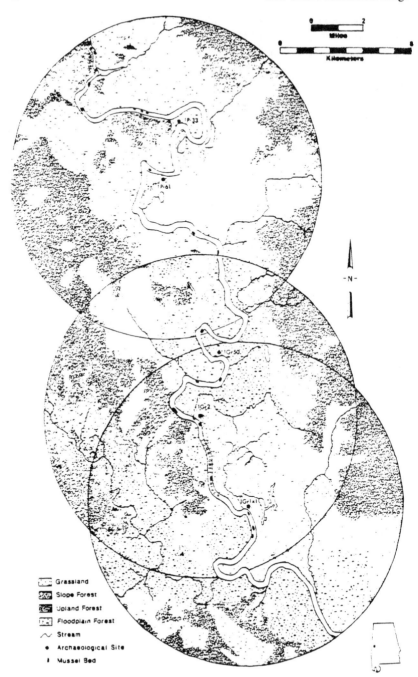

Figure 7. Vegetal Zones of the Tombigbee Drainage

The large Broken Pumpkin Creek site, for example, was located in the upland prairie near extensive forest edge and had large amounts of deer bone in its middens (Jenkins 1982, 54). During the late summer (August and September) shellfish were available in the many streams and creeks draining the wooded floodplains, and fish could be taken with hooks, nets, traps, or in weirs at this time. In the mid to late fall, deer concentrated in the slope forests, there to compete with squirrels, bear, turkey, and people for the acorn mast then available. For the people of the small Broken Pumpkin Creek slope forest camps, autumn must have been a time of plenty. During acorn season and for some time afterward, hunting would have been good, the meat animals fat, and the pelts of fur-bearing species glossy. Tons of acorns, walnuts, beechnuts, and hickory nuts could be preserved from rot and animal competitors, prepared and stored against later periods of want. As winter deepened, most animal species, deer included, sought the drier, better-drained but wooded bottomlands, leaving the wetter swampy areas to perennial waterfowl and migratory forms such as ducks and geese. That hunters from the smaller Broken Pumpkin Creek slope forest encampments sought winter game in the bottomlands is highly probable, but we have no evidence for these evanescent camps or hunting stations. Deer in particular breed in mid to late winter in slope forest or bottomland, but later they are usually driven to higher ground by the spring river rise, there to begin, with humans and other animals, yet another subsistence cycle (Severinghaus and Cheatum 1956, 83).

Settlement Pattern

The number, size, and content contrasts between upland prairie encampments and slope forest campsites have led analysts to posit a "central-based wandering" settlement pattern for peoples of the Broken Pumpkin Creek phase. As customarily understood, central-based wandering is applied to "a community that spends part of each year wandering and the rest at a settlement or 'central base,' to which it may or may not return in subsequent years" (Beardsley et al. 1956, 183). We may consider a community any group of people in which face-to-face interaction is commonplace. This description implies a population composed of two sexes and at least three biological generations, with a division of labor by both sex and age. It excludes special purpose or unisex occupation and residence groups such as mining, timbering, farming, or military parties (Murdock 1949, 79). In the Broken Pumpkin Creek case it is reasonable to view the core of a community as an aggregate of consanguineally related kinsmen capable of satisfying basic social and material needs. Although the data are far from clear on this point, most of these communities seem to have been composed of domestic groups which were the basic units of production and consumption. Each domestic group was probably responsible for hunting, harvesting, storing, and preparing its own food as well as producing and maintaining the basic tools and implements needed for day-to-day domestic life. Luxury goods of various kinds and in various quantities may have found their way to even the humblest and least competent of domestic groups, but these by no means constituted basic tools and implements, and, by any measure, were few in number. The most common intra-domestic group division of labor followed lines of age and sex, with men's tasks tending to require mobility and/or spurts of intense physical exertion (hunting, fighting, and long-distance trade). Women's work was probably long, tedious, and time consuming (shelter maintenance, pottery making, sewing, the preparation of food and clothes, and the care, early training, and nurture of children). The consanguineally related domestic groups must have been the socially stable units in the fabric of community life. It was, for instance, to and from these stable units that consumable goods—like meat; personnel, in the form of affines; and services, in the form of work or political support—must have flowed in a richly networked supradomestic unit web of rights, duties, privileges, and responsibilities. This network served to mute the potentially divisive pull of separate domestic group interests and focus attention upon broader communitywide concerns.

While the meaning given the concept of community seems clear enough, a precise construal of central-based wandering has yet to be given. There are at least three possible interpretations of the expression: (1) the entire community moved through the annual subsistence cycle as a unit, spending the greater part of each year at a central base to which they periodically returned; (2) the community broke into several domestic group aggregates for a portion of the year and then reassembled periodically at a central base; or (3) the community broke into its constituent domestic groups, each of which went its separate way for a portion of the year and then reassembled periodically at a central base. In option 1 we would expect the content of upland components to be the consequence of longer residence rather than larger groups. Slope forest and upland communities should be roughly equal in size with components of each having similar horizontal dimensions. Significant differences, if any, should lie in fewer and deeper upland components or, conversely, in more and shallower slope forests components. In option 2, we would expect smaller, shallower, and significantly more frequent slope forest components matched with larger, deeper, less-frequent upland sites. In option 3, a very large number of very small slope forest components (each being a mere trace or hint of human disturbance) should be combined with a few deep, large upland sites. The settlement pattern of the Broken Pumpkin Creek phase seems to fit option 2 the best.

Chronology

The relative chronological position of the Broken Pumpkin Creek phase is quite clear; it belongs in the Wheeler variant, which, in turn, belongs to the middle period of the Gulf Formational stage. Converting this relative date to a calendrical computation, however, will require recourse to external relationships which document the temporal position of the Wheeler ceramic series. At the Claiborne site, a Wheeler ceramic complex (composed of Wheeler Plain and Wheeler Punctated) was radiocarbon dated at 1240 B.C. and 1150 B.C. (Gagliano and Webb 1970, 69). Wheeler Plain and Punctated pottery from the Teoc Creek site in northwestern Mississippi yielded a thermoluminescence date of 1076±200 B.C. and an average radiocarbon date of 1364 B.C. (Connaway, McGahey, and Webb 1977, 107). The absence of dentate stamping, however, suggests that the Wheeler components at Claiborne and Teoc Creek are early. Dentate stamping appears later. Stratigraphic evidence at 1Lu59 indicates that dentate stamping appears as a prominent surface treatment late in the Wheeler continuum (Webb and DeJarnette 1942, 126–30). Dentate stamping appears as part of the refuge series along the Georgia–South Carolina coast between 1000 and 700 B.C. (DePratter 1975, Peterson 1970, Waring 1968). Another, and closer, occurrence of dentate stamping is to be found 100 miles to the south of Broken Pumpkin Creek territory. If Trickey's (1971, 115–28) radiometric determinations are correct, the Bayou La Batre variant peoples in the lower Tombigbee and Mobile delta were dentate stamping pottery as early as 1140±200 B.C. Thus it would appear that assigning a calendrical date of 1000 to 500 B.C. to the Broken Pumpkin Creek phase would be reasonable, if a bit conservative.

The Henson Springs Phase

Material Culture

Major modifications in pottery manufacture, an intensified use of natural resources (indicated by a greater number of base and seasonal camps and minor adjustments in their distribution), and a slow but steady growth in the social import of manipulating external sources of wealth mark the transition from the Broken Pumpkin Creek to the Henson Springs phase (DeJarnette, Walthall, and Wimberly 1975) in the upper and middle reaches of the Tombigbee drainage (fig. 8). Sand-tempered Alexander wares are diagnostic of the Henson Springs phase. In the Gainesville Lake region, at least, Alexander wares are decorated by incising and pinching. The incised motifs are usually

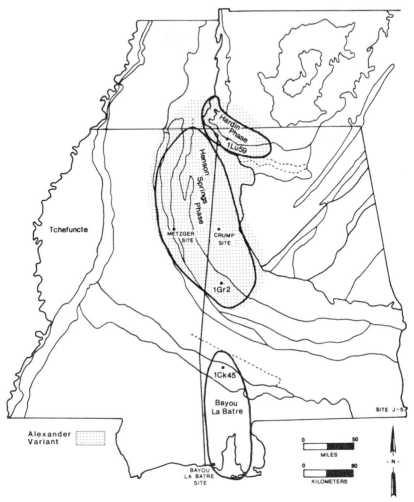

Figure 8. Selected Late Gulf Formational Sites and Manifestations

rectilinear, consisting of chevrons, chevron-filled triangles, diamonds formed
by cross-hatching, hexagons, and lines incised parallel to the rim. Curvilinear
designs, which are rare, occur in combination with rectilinear motifs (fig. 9,
B, C, D). Pinched pottery includes both fingernail punctated and pinched. The
incised and fingernail punctated pottery are Alexander Incised (fig. 9, F, G,
H, I) and Alexander Pinched types (fig. 9, A, E, J) (Haag 1939). Minority

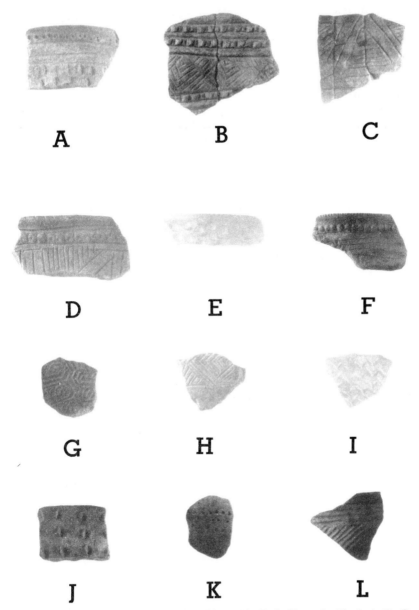

Figure 9. Pottery of the Henson Springs Phase: (A, E, J) Alexander Pinched; (B, C, D, F, G, H, I) Alexander Incised; (K) Columbus Punctated; (L) Smithsonian Zone Stamped

types include Smithsonia Zone Stamped, Columbus Punctated (fig. 9, K, L) (Heimlich 1952), Crump Punctated (DeJarnette, Walthall, and Wimberly 1975), and Reed Punctated pottery. Although the evidence is scanty, it seems that both punctated and incised pottery sherds were broken from large, flat-bottomed, straight-to-outsloping-sided vessels with excurvate rims and quadripodal supports. Nodes, or bosses, punched through from the interior immediately beneath and parallel to the lip, were a common and distinctive feature of Alexander potteries. The hole on the interior of these pieces was always smoothed over to produce an overall effect reminiscent of Havanna Hopewell wares (Griffin 1952b, 100–14). The lithic practices of Henson Springs flint-smiths suggest continuity with those of their Broken Pumpkin Creek predecessors. The predominant use of local, unheated stone continued, as did the use of exotic nonlocal stone, such as Tallahatta quartzite and Fort Payne chert (Jenkins 1982, 62). The Flint Creek type var. *Tombigbee* was the diagnostic projectile point. It was the predominant form at the Crump site where the phase was first recognized (DeJarnette, Walthall, and Wimberly 1975), has been found at 22It563 in northeastern Mississippi (personal communication from J. Bense, June 1981), and was a common form at 1Gr2, the largest Henson Springs phase component in the Gainesville reservoir (Ensor 1981).

Subsistence Practices

Subsistence data are meager at best but suggest that peoples of the Broken Pumpkin Creek and Henson Springs phases used the same basic resources: deer and nut foods, small mammals, birds, fish, and shellfish. In the central Tombigbee area, however, only hickory nuts, opossum, snake, bird, unidentified mammal, bowfin and other unidentified fish, and shellfish were found in features unequivocally assigned to Henson Springs phase components (Atkinson, Phillips, and Walling 1980, 228).

Settlement Pattern

Except for a few more base and seasonal camps per unit of space, and base camps in both prairie uplands to the west and fall line hills to the east, Henson Springs and Broken Pumpkin Creek settlement patterns were isomorphs (fig. 8). Small camps located in the slope forests probably housed transitory domestic group aggregates of limited size. Larger sites, customarily called base camps, appear to have been periodically occupied by larger, multiaggregate groups. That there seems to be more of each kind of site now may indicate either (1) population growth or (2) less intensive use of base and transitory camps. The overall picture is one of a stable population whose economic practices were finely tuned to the availability of natural foods. The rhythms of plant and animal behavior now seem to mesh well with the patterns of stability and flux in the human populations of the region (Jenkins 1982, 62–64).

Chronology

Estimates of the Henson Springs temporal position place its origin around 600 B.C.; its demise at roughly 100 B.C. This estimate is based on two radiocarbon dates from the Tombigbee drainage and relative dating with adjacent regions, where Alexander ceramics have been radiocarbon dated. Within the central reaches of the Tombigbee, material with a six-legged beaker-shaped vessel of Alexander Incised var. *Negro slough* from the Kellogg site yielded a radiocarbon date of 760±100 B.C. (Atkinson, Phillips, and Walling 1980, 195). A radiocarbon determination from 1It563, an Alexander component in the upper Tombigbee, gave a date of 360±50 B.C. (personal communication from J. Bense, June 1981). At the Sakti-Chaha site in the Tennessee valley, an Alexander midden was dated by radiocarbon to 400±75 B.C. (Dye 1980, 104). In the lower Mississippi valley, a date of 250±110 B.C. was obtained from a site containing Alexander pottery as a trade ware (Crane and Griffin 1959; Phillips 1970, 957). At the Alligator Lake site, located along the northwest coast of Florida, Alexander and Deptford pottery yielded a date of 610±80 B.C. (Lazarus 1965, 109).

A parting word about Alexander ceramics is in order at this point. Alexander potteries appear to be a combination of practices from several Middle period Gulf Formational complexes. Many Alexander elements are first found in St. Johns, Bayou La Batre, Wheeler, and possibly Thoms Creek. The most striking feature of Alexander pottery is the array of rectangular incised decorations. The origin of many of these motifs can be traced to the St. Johns pottery of Florida's transitional period (Bullen 1959, 1969, 1972). Another distinctive Alexander attribute, nodes or bosses just beneath the rim, may also be traced to St. Johns (Atkins and MacMahan 1967). The podal and annular appendages found in Alexander wares were most probably derived from Bayou La Batre, as were sand temper and coiling. Alexander ceramics have been found as minority types in the lower Mississippi valley (Ford and Quimby 1945), the northwest Florida Gulf Coast (Lazarus 1965, Willey 1949), the Alabama River (Jenkins 1981), and the Mobile Bay and delta area (Wimberly 1960), where they are associated with local ceramic complexes. Perhaps one reason for this distribution is that it developed in association with trade. The same may in fact be the case for similarities between Alexander wares and the Black Sands series of potteries well to the north (Griffin 1952b, 98–99).

3. The Woodland Stage

In the Tombigbee drainage the Woodland stage followed the Gulf Formational and preceded the Mississippian. It was marked by a continuation of the Gulf Formational pattern of hunting and foraging, modified a bit by the introduction of a few domesticates and food production of very modest proportions late in the sequence of events. Villages composed of round or oval dome-shaped timber-frame structures covered with grass, bark, or hide were to be found in the floodplain forests during the summer and fall; smaller temporary encampments were located in riverbottoms, slope forests, or uplands during the winter. The production of cord- and fabric-marked potteries; a complex mortuary ritual centered upon earthen funerary monuments which provided for the disposal of wealth and the periodic management of community labor; the widespread commitment to distinctive art styles; and a marked increase in the extent, duration, and social import of trade and barter set Woodland peoples apart (Jenkins 1982, 67–116).

Tradition

Caldwell (1958, 19–52) delineated a series of Woodland regional traditions, among them a Northern, a Middle Eastern, a Gulf, and a Southern Appalachian. The ceramic practices of his Northern and Middle Eastern traditions—that is, the production of fabric- and cord-marked ceramics—are of greatest taxonomic interest to us here. Nevertheless, it should be remembered that "these eastern cultural traditions do not on the whole represent basically different activities of their practitioners, but rather different styles of doing the same kinds of things" (Caldwell 1958, viii). What is true of all the Southeast's Woodland peoples, however, is that they were richer than their Gulf Formational predecessors, perhaps because they reaped the benefits of a deer and nut food economy enriched in the early millennia by trade and later by a few cultigens. The basic orientation throughout was, nevertheless, one of hunting and harvesting, now on a more intensive scale than ever before (see Caldwell 1958, 19–60). Food production made slow headway in the hunting and harvesting economies of the region and seems in fact to have been inhibited by the enhanced hunting efficiency that accompanied the introduction of the bow and arrow and by new and improved means of collecting, harvesting, and fishing.

Periods

We will divide the Woodland stage into Early (1000 to 100 B.C.), Middle (100 B.C. to A.D. 650), and Late (A.D. 650 to 1100) periods (Jenkins 1982, 67). Woodland remains belonging to the Early period are not found south of the fall line, hence are of little or no immediate interest to us. In our region, the years between 1000 and 100 B.C. witnessed developments attributable to the Middle and Late periods of the Gulf Formational stage. In the Tombigbee drainage, the Woodland stage opened in the Middle period (100 B.C. to A.D. 650) with the advent of newcomers who made cord- and fabric-marked ceramics and introduced new house types, burial practices, social forms, and trade goods. The early edge of the Middle period is marked by the appearance of burial mounds and fabric-marked pottery. Slightly later, cord-marked wares were added to the ceramic inventory, and the integration of local groups into the Hopewell Interaction Sphere was firmed up. This widespread sphere of interaction resulted in "striking regional differences in the secular, domestic and non-mortuary aspects . . . and an interesting if short list of exact similarities in funerary usages and mortuary artifacts over great distances" (Caldwell 1964, 138). In the Tombigbee drainage there were many burial mounds containing nonlocal items like silver-plated panpipes, galena, copper, platform pipes, greenstone celts, trade pots, and projectile points of foreign make (Bohannon 1972, Cotter and Corbett 1951, Jennings 1941). The Late period (A.D. 600 to 1100) was marked by a rapidly expanding population as evidenced by more and larger riverbottom middens, a simplification of burial ritual, and the lapse of those extensive trade contacts embedded in the Hopewell Interaction Sphere. Weeden Island ceremonialism was in full swing and had spread from its northern Florida homeland to groups in southern Georgia and Alabama, but it was a weak reflection, at best, of its northern (i.e., Hopewell) counterpart.

Variants

The Tombigbee drainage was home to two temporal variants during the
Woodland stage. The earliest of these, the Miller variant, flourished during the
Middle period (100 B.C. to A.D. 600); the later, or Baytown, variant spanned
the years from A.D. 600 to 1100. All available evidence suggests that peoples
of the Miller variant moved into the Tombigbee drainage from the north (fig.
10), bringing with them elements of a new lifestyle built around the manipulation of externally derived forms of durable wealth and the management of

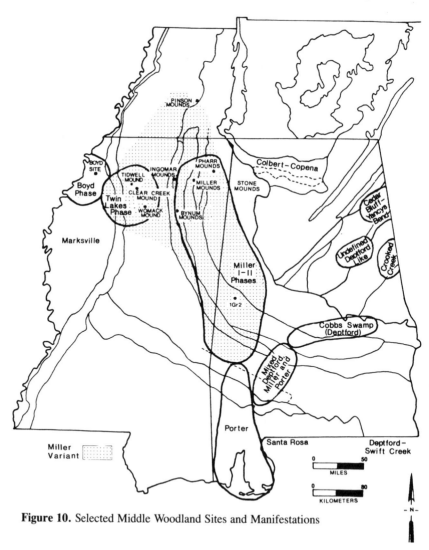

Figure 10. Selected Middle Woodland Sites and Manifestations

Figure 11. Artifacts and Features of the Miller Variant

labor temporarily but periodically committed to preparing for public mortuary ceremonies (Jenkins 1982, 69). The newcomers made fabric-marked pottery of the Saltillo type, produced a plain ware of the Baldwin type, and later added cord-marked wares of the Furrs type to their ceramic inventory (fig. 11).

Their flint knappers produced lanceolate-expanded haft projectiles of the Mud Creek type and lanceolate spike points of the Bradley type. Small, seasonally occupied villages, clusters of large round or oval (35 to 70 feet in longest axis) timber-framed bark-, grass-, or hide-covered houses, were now to be found on suitable stretches of bottomland not far from public monuments of mounded earth containing the remains of the group's ancestors and providing evidence of its success in manipulating external sources of durable wealth. Smaller, more dispersed encampments bespeak a seasonal round regulated by the continuing need to move people to huntable and harvestable natural foods (Jenkins 1982, 68–98). On the whole, however, Miller variant peoples seem less precariously established than their Alexander variant predecessors. This impression may, of course, be more apparent than real. The appearance of stability is conveyed by the stylistic precocity of ceramic productions, the consumption of wealth in burial ritual, and the creation of community monuments in the form of burial tumulii. The mortuary monuments in and of themselves seem to indicate a commitment to forms of social, economic, and political life having a firmer structure than their Gulf Formational forerunners. It seems that internal ranking was emerging, that there were men in these Miller communities who could channel the flow of wealth made available through trade and could command community resources, albeit temporarily.

The Woodland populations of the Southeast began a rather rapid expansion by about A.D. 400, and by A.D. 600 the region was well peopled; contacts with Hopewellians had diminished, if not collapsed; Weeden Island ceremonialism was spreading northward and westward; and the Baytown variant succeeded its Miller progenitor in the Tombigbee drainage (fig. 12). The Baytown variant was characterized by grog-tempered ware of the Baytown, Withers, and Alligator Incised and Mulberry Creek Cord Marked types (fig. 13). Baytown variant lithic technology was marked by the appearance of small triangular projectile points of the Madison, Hamilton, and Pickens types. Nut foods and other biotic collectibles retained their import, while dependence upon smaller mammals, reptiles, fish, and shellfish increased. Small quantities of maize were grown in late Baytown times, especially in those regions in which sedentary life and larger group size prevailed. Baytown peoples cultivated little compared with their Mississippian successors, but the cultivation that did occur laid the foundation for later incorporation into a lifeway built around the needs of food production. Mortuary ritual was simplified, there was a lapse in the construction of community mortuary monuments (i.e., burial tumulli), and we suppose a lapse in the temporary command over benefits and resources that construction of earth-covered tombs required. The dead were interred in shallow graves (rectangular, oval, or circular holes in the ground) and were accompanied by modest grave goods, if any at all (fig. 13) (Jenkins 1982, 99–115).

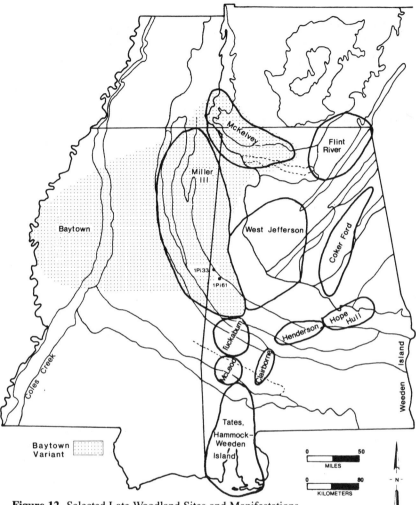

Figure 12. Selected Late Woodland Sites and Manifestations

Horizon

To recapitulate, our taxonomic edifice consists of a Woodland stage divided into three sequent periods (Early, from 1000 B.C. to A.D. 100; Middle, from A.D. 100 to A.D. 600; and Late, from A.D. 600 to A.D. 1100). The later two are of taxonomic relevance in the Tombigbee drainage. The Middle period hosted the Miller variant, and the Later period the Baytown variant. Miller variant remains were created by a vigorous immigrant population whose human po-

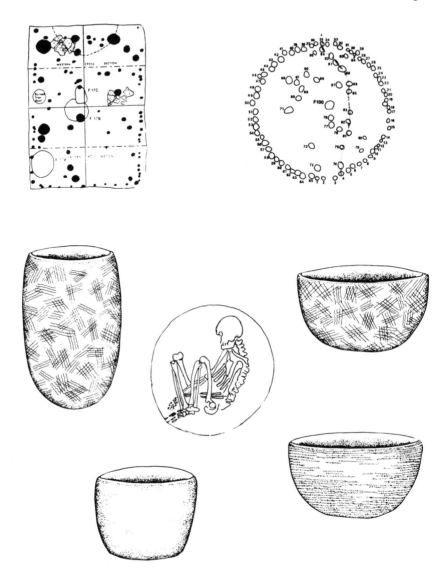

Figure 13. Artifacts and Features of the Baytown Variant

tentials were in dynamic equilibrium with the region's huntable and collectible food supply. Throughout the span of the Miller variant, participation in the Hopewell Interaction Sphere gave form to an emergent emphasis upon social ranking and counteracted the centrifugal pull of local adaptations which had shaped the previous course of human affairs. Thus, the Hopewell Interaction Sphere was a horizon for the Middle period, a channel for the exchange of ideas and goods which countermanded the forces of regionalism. As we shall see shortly, the phases in the Miller variant were integrated through the Northern and Middle Eastern ceramic traditions first proposed by Caldwell (1958, 19–34). These two ceramic traditions also ran through and united the Miller variant with its Baytown successor. The peoples who produced the Baytown variant were, however, more numerous than their Miller ancestors, pressed harder on the available supplies of natural foods, were a bit more sedentary, and, in overall adjustment to their environment, were in metastable equilibrium. The centripetal tug of the Hopewell Interaction Sphere had lapsed and the pull of regionalism had reasserted itself and was growing in strength, but the external force which, ultimately, tipped the balance to full-scale food production was the advent of Mississippians. We shall discuss this issue in detail later. First we must turn to the subregional and subareal taxonomic structure of the Woodland stage.

The Miller One Phase

Material Culture

The Miller One phase was the earliest Miller variant manifestation in the central and upper Tombigbee drainages. Miller One peoples were, however, immigrants whose closest cultural heirs and relatives were found to the north. Saltillo Fabric Marked (fig. 14, G, I, K) and Baldwin Plain (excluding var. *Oneal*) were the dominant Miller One potteries, although Furrs Cord Marked (fig. 14, E, F, H, J) was later added to the ceramic inventory. There were a few minor differences in Baldwin Plain vessel shape that were either spatially or temporally significant. In the Miller components excavated by Cotter and Corbett (1951, 17) at the Bynum site (fig. 15), a deep hemispherical bowl with a rim that met the vessel wall at a right angle was the dominant form. This form was also found in Miller components at the Pharr site (Bohannon 1972, 26). Nevertheless, the sharply everted rim was rare in Miller components farther south. The upper Tombigbee Baldwin Plain with everted rim was therefore typed as variety Baldwin, while its noneverted rim counterpart to the south was typed as variety Blubber. Vessels of Saltillo Fabric Marked show even less variability than those of the Baldwin type. The only vessel shape

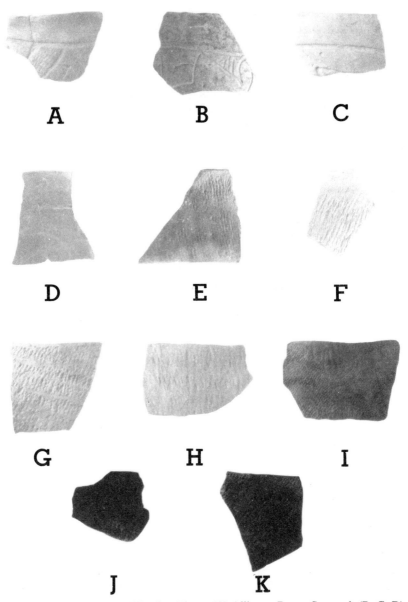

Figure 14. Pottery of the Miller One Phase: (A) Alligator Bayou Stamped; (B, C, D) Basin Bayou Incised; (E, F, H, J) Furrs Cord Marked; (G, I, K) Saltillo Fabric Marked

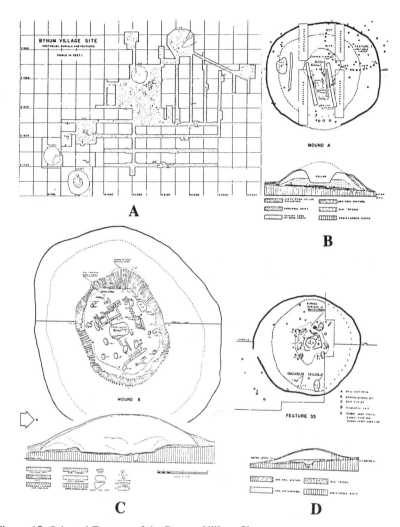

Figure 15. Selected Features of the Bynum Village Site

known is the large conoidal jar with straight to gently outflaring rim (Cotter and Corbett 1951, 18). The major vessel shape for Furrs Cord Marked was a conoidal to slightly globular jar with a direct or gently inslanting rim. None of these vessel forms occurred with appendages.

Miller One phase projectile points have been grouped into two morphology based clusters—the lanceolate expanded haft and the lanceolate spike. Points of the expanded haft cluster had excurvate or straight-blade edges. The most prominent type was the Mud Creek Point (Ensor 1981, 152–56) found at the Bynum site (Cotter and Corbett 1951, plates 10 and 13), the Okashua site (Wynn and Atkinson 1976, plate 6), and 1Gr2 (Ensor 1981). The Bradley spike point was the major type of the lanceolate spike cluster. They were narrow, thick, lancelike forms with constricting, excurvate bases, like those found at 1Gr2 and 1Pi61. Miller One phase stonesmiths understood the advantages of heat treating the local nodular cherts of the Tombigbee gravel bars. Heat treating became an integral procedure in the manufacture of both projectile points and other stone tools. The success of heat treating may, in fact, explain the dramatic drop in the use of exotic stone that occurred in Miller One times (Ensor 1980, 84–87).

Settlement Pattern and Ceremonialism

Sites attributed to the Miller One phase are either small temporary encampments; larger, semisedentary settlements; or earthen burial monuments. The last two frequently co-occur in non-floodplain contexts (Jenkins 1982, 72). The burial monuments are the most impressive of the Miller One phase sites, for they afford a glimpse of the rich ceremonialism that periodically allowed nascent authorities to command community benefits and resources. Within the upper Tombigbee drainage, two mound clusters, Bynum and Pharr, were excavated. The artifacts from both indicate active participation in Hopewellian ceremonialism. At both the Bynum and Pharr mounds foreign ceramics, worked copper, galena, and nonlocal chert suggest contact with a panregional trade system. The location of both sites on the Natchez Trace has even led some to argue that it served as a trade route as early as Hopewellian times (see Myer 1928, 811).

Three of the five excavated mounds at the Bynum site yielded significant information on Miller One ceremonialism (Cotter and Corbett 1951, 1). Mound A, for instance, contained in its center two horizontal parallel logs, lying on a burned platform. Two extended and three flexed burials lay upon the platform between the logs (fig. 15, B). One of these bodies was adorned with a pair of double cymbal-type copper earspools; the other three were *in situ* cremations (Cotter and Corbett 1951, 6). The center of a second mound contained a large oval excavation, around the outside edge of which were numerous small parallel logs. Sixteen large posts were set in the floor of the oval excavation; they were all that remained of a charnel house built in and over it (fig. 15, C). A small hole had been dug through the bottom of the excavated charnel house floor, lined with clay, then used as a crematorium—a task that left the pit walls a bright brick red. On the excavated floor of the charnel house were three human cremations intermixed with ash and accompanied by an L-shaped row of twenty-nine stone celts and a cluster of nine Snyders points. A flesh burial lay on its back near the eastern edge of the excavated floor. The floor fill itself contained two pairs of copper earspools, a lump of galena, and two fragments of marine shell. The crematory pit contained a cremation and a cluster of eight Snyder points (Cotter and Corbett 1951, plate 5). Because none of the artifacts in the charnel house floor fill or in the crematory pit was fire damaged, Cotter and Corbett (1951, 8) concluded that they and the flesh burial were included after the charnal house was burned. The center of a third mound contained a rectangular excavation with a series of small parallel logs around its western edge. A charnel house, supported by a frame of four stout posts, was set over the excavation floor and a smaller circular crematory pit, which contained the remains of an undetermined number of people, was dug into it (fig. 15, D). A single polished celt lay on the charnel house floor; a copper earspool and a rolled copper bead were taken from the crematory pit (Cotter and Corbett 1951, 9).

Of the eight mounds at the Pharr site, all four excavated by Bohannon (1972) were of Miller One (Pharr subphase) authorship. One of them, a conical mound, contained a central crematory, a simple, rectangular, flat-bottomed pit which held three thin lenses of calcined human bone and charcoal. A second conical mound also contained a centrally located crematory, in this case an oval excavation, dug into a prepared burned mound base, which had been paved with flat sandstone slabs. A broken copper spool and a few fragments of burned human bone were found on the paving. A burial consisting of a crumbled skull accompanied by two copper spools lay beyond the pavement's edge (Bohannon 1972, 13–14). The third mound excavated was a bit more complex. It had been built in three stages, but the first stage seems to have been the most elaborate. It consisted of a low, centrally located platform, with its upper surface marked by a circular crematory, and two rectangular pits. A miniature Marksville Incised var. *Marksville* vessel sat at the edge of the crematory. Other ceramics found on the platform surface were a miniature Flint River Brushed vessel, three miniature sand-tempered zone-stamped vessels, one miniature Baldwin Plain pot, and a partial Saltillo Fabric Marked pot. Other artifacts from the platform surface included a slab of wood covered with copper sheeting, a silver sheet-plated panpipe, and a burned stone. One of the rectangular holes through the platform contained a cache of points resembling those of the lanceolate spike cluster (Ensor, 1981). Two rectangular pits were found on the edge of the platform, one containing a miniature sand-tempered zone-stamped vessel and a miniature Flint River Brushed jar, the other a miniature Flint River Cord Marked pot. The fourth excavated mound contained only a clean, rectangular, fired basin. Although no artifacts or fragmentary bones were found in this feature, it was almost certainly a crematory.

To summarize the mortuary monument data, during Miller One phase times (particularly during the Bynum and Pharr subphases) there were at least three different burial programs with their separate facilities in use—the charnel house, the burial crypt, and the platform. Most numerous were the charnel house and burial crypt. The charnel house was characterized by Brown (1979, 212) as a structure "designed to shelter both the dead and associated mortuary processing activities. Specific space was allocated to burials and a crematory basin was located inside." Good examples of charnel houses were found at Bynum; probable charnel houses were found at Pharr. The crypt was a different type of facility. As described by Brown (1979, 211–12), "the Hopewell crypt is a large box constructed for storage of the dead and their grave goods and little else. At the death of an individual the corpse was placed in this facility and accorded no further attention unless the skeletal remains were gathered later into a bundle or dumped outside." A crypt was found at the Bynum site. The third facility, a platform, consisted of an earthen bench which had a crematory on it and holes dug through it which contained the cremated remains. When the platform had received the last of its dead, it was covered over with a layer of earth, as indicated by one of the mounds at the Pharr site. Brown (1979, 218–19) argues that the charnel house was most common in Ohio Hopewell burial programs; the platform appeared sporadically as far north as Ontario (Johnston 1968) and as far south as Louisiana (Ford and Willey 1940), and the crypt was most common in Illinois Hopewell. Given this distribution, Miller One phase ceremonialism seems more closely related to Ohio than to Illinois Hopewell (Jenkins 1982, 76).

Subsistence Practices

Semisedentary Miller One settlements appear in upland prairie, slope forest, or floodplains well away from periodically inundated areas and on fine sands (Jenkins, Curren, and DeLeon 1975). They invariably contain a dark, organically stained midden with rich lithic and ceramic accompaniments. Ceramics usually outnumber lithics at any given site. Shellfish remains, butchered and unbutchered bone, plant remains, and other detritus of day-to-day life complete the midden inventory. An analysis of the faunal and floral remains from a midden at 1Gr2 suggests a summer or late summer through late fall sedentary season, with a winter to spring foraging season (Caddell 1981a, 32). During the sedentary season, sustenance was derived from the harvest of floodplain forest products, the hunting of deer, and the taking of shellfish, fish, and turtles from rivers and sloughs. The best data on sedentary season housing are from the 2.8 hectare village associated with the six Bynum mounds (Cotter and Corbett 1951). Seven circular or ovate house patterns (measuring from 35 to 78 feet in diameter) were found, all in a northwest to southeast line across the site (fig. 15, A). A pole-supported bark-, thatch-, and/or hide-covered dome-shaped structure with central hearth is indicated. An eighth and later structure was built at the site during Miller Three phase times (Cotter and Corbett 1951, 11–14). At the Okashua site, several concentrations of postholes were interpreted as the remains of lean-to-like habitations (Wynn and Atkinson 1976, fig. 15), but this construal is, as yet, questionable.

During the winter forage, Miller One communities broke into smaller aggregates of kinsmen intent upon hunting and taking advantage of dispersed stands of natural foods. Their transitory camps are marked by sparse scatters of ceramics and lithics (with the latter predominating) and the total absence of middens containing the offal of day-to-day existence (Jenkins 1982, 73).

Prior to the survey and mitigation accompanying construction of the Tennessee-Tombigbee Waterway, knowledge of the spatial spread of the Miller One phase was restricted (see Bohannon 1972, Cotter and Corbett 1951, Jennings 1941 and 1944). Most considered the Miller variant a localized northeastern Mississippi phenomenon. William Sears was a major exception, for after surveying the lower Tombigbee in 1957 and 1969, he recognized that Miller variant ceramics were to be found as far south as the Breckenridge landing mounds (Moore 1901), 25 miles south of Demopolis, Alabama (Sears 1977, 160–61). In fact, recent work along the Tombigbee indicates a Miller One phase presence as far south as Horse Creek, 40 miles south of Demopolis (Brose, Jenkins, and Weisman 1982). The northern boundary seems to be the headwaters of the Tombigbee, that is, if the Pharr mounds site contains the northernmost Miller One component. The western boundary appears to be near the Tombigbee's headwater creeks; the eastern limit seems to be the Warrior River south of the fall line (fig. 12) (Jenkins 1982, 77).

Chronology and Subphases

The Miller One phase flourished in the four centuries between 100 B.C. and A.D. 300. The phase has been divided, however, into three temporally sequent subphases (Bynum, Pharr, and Craigs Landing) on the basis of variations in the frequency of ceramic types and varieties (fig. 16). All of the pottery manufactured during the Bynum subphase can be typed as Baldwin Plain or Saltillo Fabric Marked. The Bynum subphase is best represented at the Bynum mound site (by Mound D) and at 22Le353 (Jennings 1941, 205). At the Bynum site, Baldwin Plain comprised 76.1 percent and Saltillo Fabric Marked 22.6 percent of the total ceramic content of Mound B. Although radiocarbon dates are unavailable, the Bynum subphase can (by reference to ceramic style

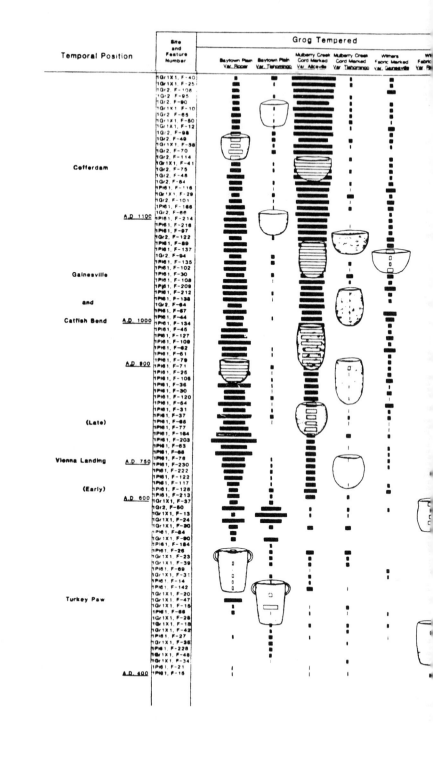

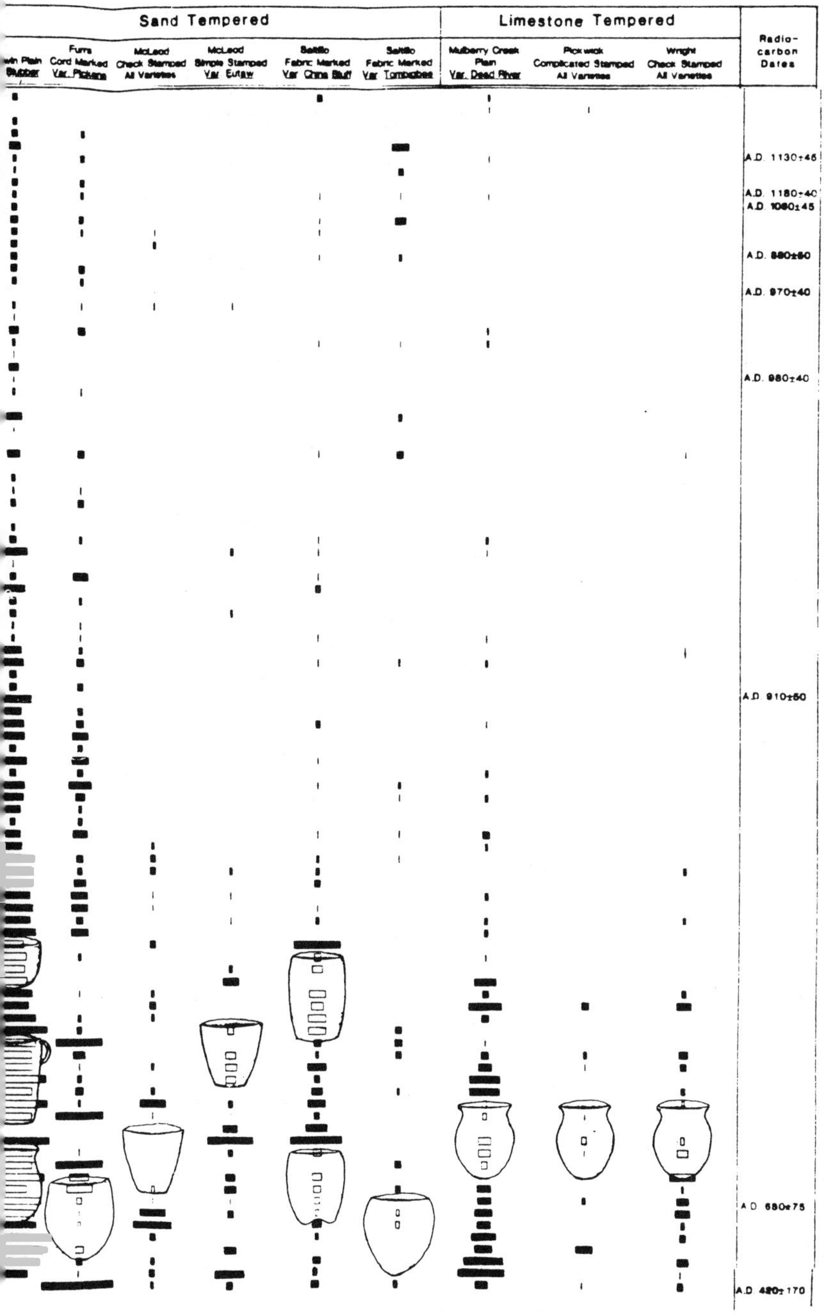

Figure 16. Seriation of Late Middle Woodland and Late Woodland Ceramics from the Gainesville Lake Area

congruity and cross-dating) be estimated at 100 B.C. to A.D. 1 (Jenkins 1982, 69; Phillips 1970, 878).

The Pharr subphase is defined by the initial appearance of Furrs Cord Marked and its addition to a complex which includes Baldwin Plain and Saltillo Fabric Marked. Other minority types now include Basin Bayou Incised (fig. 14, B, C, D), Alligator Bayou Stamped (fig. 14, A), and possibly Mound Field Net Marked. These minority types are, of course, far more common in the Middle Woodland complexes of the lower Tombigbee, Mobile Bay, and northwestern Florida regions (Wimberly 1960, Willey 1949). After its initial appearance, Furrs Cord Marked increased in frequency until it became a major type. During the Pharr subphase, however, Furrs Cord Marked accounted for no more than 12 percent of the ceramics manufactured. Pharr subphase components have been excavated at the Pharr site (Bohannon 1972), Mounds A and B at the Bynum site (Cotter and Corbett 1951) and at 1Gr2 in the Gainesville Lake area (Jenkins and Ensor 1981). The Craigs Landing subphase is characterized by an increase in the relative amount of Furrs Cord Marked Pottery. The most thoroughly excavated component of the subphase was at 1Gr2, the Craigs Landing site, where a compact midden 40 to 50 feet in diameter was encountered. The midden was 6 to 8 inches thick and lay beneath a Miller Three phase component (Jenkins 1982, 70). The ceramics within the midden consisted of 40 percent Baldwin Plain var. *Blubber,* 36 percent Saltillo Fabric Marked var. *Tombigbee,* and 20 percent Furrs Cord Marked var. *Pickens.* Minority types found with greater frequency to the south (Wimberly 1960) include Basin Bayou Incised vars. *River Bend, Fenache Creek,* and *West Greene;* Santa Rosa Stamped var. *unspecified;* and Alligator Bayou Stamped vars. *Sumter, Boguechitto,* and *Goodson's Ferry.* Together, these minority types form less than 3 percent of the Craigs Landing ceramic complex. Five trade sherds of Marksville Stamped var. *unspecified* indicate a date between A.D. 200 and 400, based on analogous types dated in the lower Mississippi valley (Phillips 1970, 111; Toth 1979, 194). Thus, increased amounts of Furrs Cord Marked, from 12 to 20 percent, and cross-dating with Marksville Stamped materials both indicate that a Craigs Landing subphase date of A.D. 100 to 300 would be reasonable (Jenkins 1982, 70).

The Miller Two Phase

Material Culture

The Miller Two phase was a direct development from the Craigs Landing subphase of Miller One. It is marked by a decline in the popularity of Saltillo Fabric Marked pottery and a growth in the popularity of Baldwin Plain and

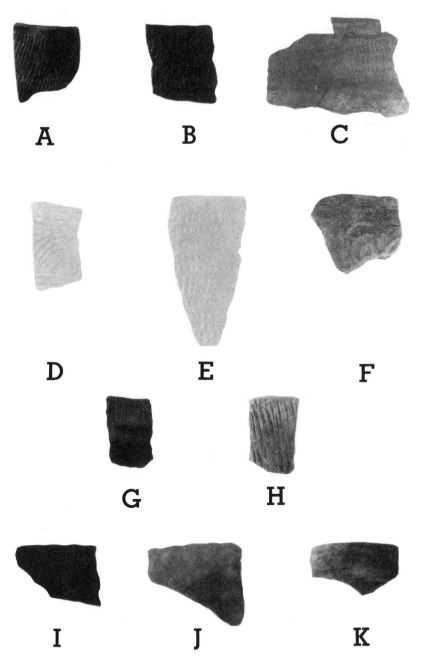

Figure 17. Pottery of the Miller Two Phase: (A, B, G, H) Furrs Cord Marked; (C, E) Saltillo Fabric Marked; (D, F) Swift Creek Complicated Stamped; (I, J, K) Baldwin Plain

Furrs Cord Marked potteries (fig. 17). In fact, Baldwin Plain and Furrs Cord Marked wares now become the dominant types, and by the end of the phase, grog, which had previously been unimportant, rivaled the popularity of sand as a temper. The Limestone Tempered Mulberry Creek Plain and Flint River Cord Marked wares are present in a minority early in the phase; the Sand Tempered Simple Stamped, McLeod Check Stamped, grog-tempered Baytown Plain, Withers Fabric Marked and bone-tempered Turkey Paw Plain and Fabric Marked are characteristic minority types later. The vessel forms represented include large hemispherical bowls, large and small flat-bottomed beakers with outsloping sides, large conoidal jars with straight to gently outflaring rims, conoidal to slightly globular jars with a direct or gently insloping rim, and large straight-sided flat-bottomed vessels that occasionally carry large crude loop handles riveted to the vessel wall (Jenkins 1982, 85–89).

The lithics of the Miller Two phase include Tombigbee stemmed types, defined by their straight to contracting haft element and tapered shoulders. Two varieties, *Tombigbee* and *Turkey Paw,* can be recognized; the former by its straight edges, tapered shoulder, and parallel haft elements; the latter by its excurvate to straight blade edges, tapered shoulder, and straight basal edge (Ensor 1981).

In the later years of the Miller Two phase, projectile points and other stone tools were made from large flakes drawn from heat-treated local cobbles. Thermal spalls are a common component of the lithic debitage, 95 percent of which shows thermal alteration. Imitative experiments indicate that the cobbles were heated to between 300 and 400 degrees centigrade, at which interval they turned dull pinkish red. After heating, the cobbles were reduced by wood or bone pressure or percussion flaking (stone on stone bipolar flaking had, for all intents and purposes, disappeared) to form the large cobble preforms, blanks, projectile points, and cores found in the later Miller Two sites (Ensor 1980, 83–90; Ensor 1981). The major tool groups produced from these preforms, blanks, and cores included flake scrapers, unifacially chipped perforators, and unifacial and bifacial edge-trimmed cutting tools (Jenkins 1982, 89–90).

Settlement Pattern and Subsistence Practices

The Miller Two subsistence-settlement system was a minimally modified copy of its Miller One progenitor. Miller Two populations formed semisedentary base camp aggregates during the summer and early fall. These, like their Miller One prototypes, were settlements composed of round or oval timberframe structures covered with grass, bark, or hide and located in riverine floodplain/forest contexts. During excavations at the Miller site, for instance,

Jennings (1941) found the remains of two round and two oval houses. The round structures were 20 feet in diameter; the oval examples measured 15 by 18 feet. These structures, which were probably domed and may have been thatched, were built of individually set posts, 0.3 to 0.5 foot in diameter, set on the average 1.2 feet apart. Examples of later Miller Two houses were found at 1Gr1x1 and 1Gr2. Site 1Gr1x1 contained an oval structure 36 feet long and 29 feet wide, with two earth ovens, one centrally located, the other situated near a presumed north entrance (fig. 18). Four large posts (averaging 1.5 feet in diameter) were set in a square around the centrally located oven; the walls had a superstructure of individually set posts averaging 0.08 foot in diameter. An arc of ash and burned grass around the southern perimeter of the structure may have been the remains of wall and/or roof thatch. One other pit was found inside the structure and eight more were located on its outer edge (Jenkins and Ensor 1981, fig. 19).

In addition to the remains of houses, these base camps contained pits and middens filled with the offal of day-to-day existence. At 1Gr1x1, 1Gr2, and 1Pi61, hickory nut shells were found in all features. They were, in fact, the most abundant nut remains. Acorns were next in frequency, and walnuts were least abundant. Weed seeds, a natural by-product of a cleared and otherwise human disturbed habitat, included pigweed, may grass, partridge peas, pokeweed, sumac, fescue, goosefoot, wood sorrel, and dove weed. It is, of course, possible that although induced by human habitat disturbances, parts of

Figure 18. Artist's Recreation of Oval Woodland House Based upon Evidence from Site 1Gr1x1

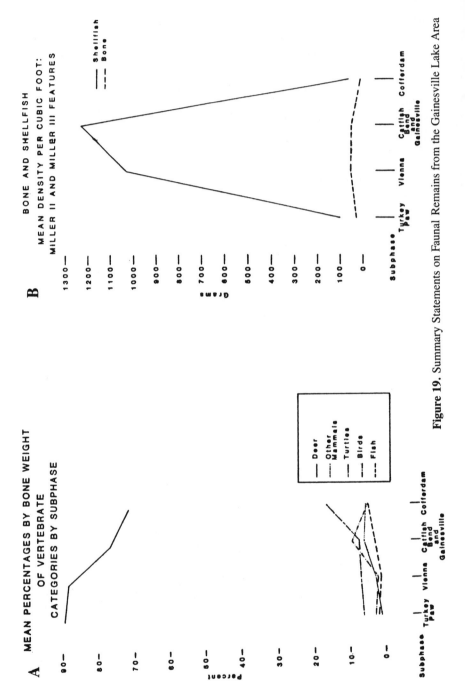

Figure 19. Summary Statements on Faunal Remains from the Gainesville Lake Area

these plants were gathered for food, for use as medicines, or as raw material for the manufacture of fiber-based products. Other plants, such as persimmon, grape, honey locust, palmetto, and hawthorne were less easily spread by natural means. Parts of these plants were found in the daily detritus of base-camp life because they were gathered for food (Caddell 1981a).

If excavated base-camp remains are indicative, the Miller One phase dependence on deer had waned by Miller Two times. The amount of deer bone per sample, for instance, dropped to 89 percent by weight, while the weight of other mammal bone per sample grew to 11 percent (fig. 19, A). Now, too, there is an interesting diversification of fauna in base-camp assemblages. Next to deer, the most important game animals were fish (14 percent), turtles (6.2 percent), turkey (4.4 percent), squirrel (1.7 percent), and raccoon (2.9 percent). Animals that occur in frequencies of less than 1 percent include opossum, beaver, dog, gray fox, black bear, skunk, and cougar (Woodrick 1981, tables 37 and 38). In addition to diversification, there seems to have been an emergent trend in Miller Two times toward greater dependence on second-line resources (i.e., those whose procurement and preparation cost is higher per calorie yield than first-line resources). This perhaps is an early warning sign of emergent problems in the balance between food supply and population growth (Jenkins 1982, 90–98).

The faunal and floral remains indicate a summer through fall occupation for base camps. During the winter, Miller Two populations split into smaller foraging groups just as their Miller One ancestors had. Now, however, there seem to be more winter foraging encampments per unit of territory. Jenkins (1982, 90–98), for example, identified eighteen transitory foraging camps in the Gainesville Lake area. These sites contained sparse scatters of ceramics and lithics (with the latter predominating). Like their earlier counterparts, they lacked middens containing the offal of day-to-day existence and most probably contained evidence of only temporary shelters, if there were any at all. It should be noted that Jenkins (1982, 99) urges caution in assessing these sites, for some could belong to Miller Three rather than to Miller Two.

Ceremonialism

Jennings excavated two mounds representing the simplified burial ritual of Miller Two times. One of these, Mound A at the Miller site, was a conical accretional structure 4.5 m (15 ft.) high. It contained the remains of thirty-two individuals, most singly interred but some buried together. Two adults, for example, were laid out together on the mound floor near its center. The remaining interments, either flexed or extended (with the latter predominating), were mound fill inclusions. A few grave goods were buried with the dead: a

carved limestone platform pipe and a conch shell were near the head of one of
the two centrally located adults; eight stemmed elongated points or knives, a
vessel fragment, a terrapin carapace, and a pair of copper earspools were
distributed among the remainder of the deceased (Jennings 1941, 190–91).
The second structure, Mound B, was 4 m (13 ft.) high with a 24-m (80-ft.)
basal diameter. It contained six primary inhumations, three of which lay in
shallow pits beneath the mound, the remainder in a cluster near the mound
center, 5 feet above its floor. A Furrs Cord Marked vessel was associated with
the submound pit burials; a crushed Baldwin Plain jar, with the mound fill
interments (Jennings 1941, 190–91; 194–95). Moore (1901) located and tested a large number of burial mounds within the central and lower Tombigbee
valley that date to the Miller Two phase. The few artifacts from these mounds
include stone celts, chert bifaces, and caches of cobbles (Jenkins 1979, 179–
88). Miller Two burials show fewer exotic or nonlocal artifacts and less elaborate preparation than previously.

The geographic distribution of Miller Two phase remains resembles that of
its Miller One phase ancestor. The northern reaches of Miller Two territory lie
in the upper Tombigbee (Atkinson 1978, Blakeman 1976, Hubbert 1978). To
the south, a recent reconnaissance of the lower Tombigbee has identified Miller Two base camps in the Southern Red Hills about 30 miles below Demopolis (Jenkins 1981, 95). To the east, a few Miller Two components may be
found in the Black Warrior drainage, but these are small and could represent
task specific encampments of peoples based in nearby sections of the Tombigbee (Jenkins 1982, 95) . Numerous Miller-like sites similar to Womack
(Koehler 1966) may be found on and east of the Tombigbee–Mississippi River
divide, but the western limit of the phase is not yet clear (fig. 12). Miller Two
will probably be found to overlap artifactually and spatially with the Late
Twin Lakes phase (Phillips 1970, 891–92).

Chronology and Subphases

Calendrical dates for the Miller Two phase may be estimated by using ceramic cross-finds and radiocarbon determinations. The early edge of the phase
lies in the years between A.D. 300 and A.D. 400 (i.e., the same as the end of
the Miller One phase, Craigs Landing subphase) based on radiocarbon dated
at the Cofferdam site (Blakeman 1975). Three radiocarbon determinations
suggest a midrange date of A.D. 450 and a terminal date in the late 600s or
early 700s. The earliest date (A.D. 420±170) from the Gainesville Lake area
approximates the midpoint of the phase as does a later determination of A.D.
490±50. An A.D. 680±75 assay apparently dates the later part of the phase.
Ceramic cross-finds from Copena sites in the Tennessee valley and from

McLeod and early Weeden Island complexes support the few radiometric assays now available (see Jenkins 1982, 95–98).

The Miller Two phase has been divided into an early Tupelo and later Turkey Paw subphase. The earliest, or Tupelo, subphase is not well understood, its best excavated example being the Miller mound site MLe63 (Jennings 1941). The ceramics from this site suggest that Tupelo subphase components should contain roughly 50 percent Furrs Cord Marked, 10 to 15 percent Saltillo Fabric Marked, and 35 to 40 percent Baldwin Plain. Minority wares should include Mulberry Creek Plain and Flint River Cord Marked (Jenkins 1982, 85). The Tupelo subphase is presumed to have flourished for the century and a half between A.D. 300 and 450.

Three components in the Gainesville Lake area, 1Gr1x1, 1Gr2, and 1Pi61, provide the basic data for defining the Turkey Paw subphase. During this subphase, sand-tempered wares are dominant although in decline. Baldwin Plain var. *Blubber* ranges in frequency from 20 to 60 percent, with a mean of 40 percent. The next most popular sand-tempered ware is Saltillo Fabric Marked var. *China Bluff*, which ranges from 10 to 15 percent of the total ceramic complex. Saltillo Fabric Marked var. *China Bluff*, like Withers Fabric Marked vars. *River Bend* and *Montgomery*, has a cord-wrapped rod-impressed surface; it occurs only sporadically before and after the Turkey Paw subphase. Hence, if found in some numbers, sherds of this type are a good subphase marker. The next most numerous variety of sand-tempered pottery is Furrs Cord Marked var. *Pickens*, which averages 2 to 6 percent. Two ceramic types diagnostic of the McLeod complex also appear in the sand-tempered wares of Turkey Paw times (see Wimberly 1960). The most numerous of these is McLeod Simple Stamped var. *Eutaw* with an average frequency of less than 10 percent. McLeod Check Stamped var. *Bigbee* has an average range of 3 to 6 percent. Other sand-tempered minority types, indicative perhaps of extralocal contacts, include Weeden Island Red Filmed, Late Swift Creek Complicated Stamped (fig. 17, D, F), Carabelle Punctated and Incised, McLeod Linear Check Stamped and Basin Bayou Incised (fig. 16). Together, these minority types constitute less than 2 percent of the Turkey Paw ceramic complex (Jenkins 1982, 87–89).

Grog-tempered ware was less popular early, comprising only 5 percent of the ceramic inventory in the early years, but increased in popularity later, ultimately challenging sand-tempered wares for dominance. Baldwin Plain var. *Tishomingo*, for instance, grew in popularity as did the grog-tempered var. *Roper*. By the end of the Turkey Paw subphase, grog and sand temper appeared with roughly equal frequency. Baytown Plain is the dominant grog-tempered pottery type. Cord-roughened surface treatments are found on several Turkey Paw grog-tempered wares, Mulberry Creek Cord Marked var. *Aliceville* (with dense grog), and var. *Tishomingo* (with sparse grog) among them. Fabric-marked grog-tempered wares now include Withers Fabric Marked vars. *Craigs Landing, Montgomery, River Bend,* and *Gainesville.* Grog-tempered minority types which have a collective frequency of less than 2 percent are Wheeler Check Stamped var. *Sipsey,* Yeates Net Impressed var. *Yeates,* Gainesville Complicated Stamped var. *Gainesville,* and Marksville Incised var. *Yokena* (fig. 16) (Jenkins 1982, 87–89).

Other Turkey Paw subphase ceramic types are either limestone or bone tempered, with limestone being a more frequent aplastic inclusion than bone. Mulberry Creek Plain var. *Dead River* is the most numerous variety of the limestone-tempered group. It is most popular early in the subphase and declines in frequency later. Wright Check Stamped is the second most numerous limestone-tempered type, occurring in vars. *Wheeler Bend* and *Dead River* and averaging less than 10 percent. The least frequent limestone-tempered type is Pickwick Complicated Stamped vars. *Coal Fire* and *Hogeye.* The bone-tempered wares occur most frequently in two varieties: Turkey Paw

Table 1.   *Gainesville Lake Area Radiocarbon Dates*

Feature	Sample No.	Date (A.D.)	Phase
Site 1Pi61			
92 (Structure 4)	1002	1030 ± 55	Terminal Miller III
17 (Structure 1)	1003	1240 ± 80	Terminal Miller III
15	1005	420 ± 170	Late Miller II
25	1004	910 ± 50	Early Miller III
Site 1Gr1x1			
42	1001	680 ± 75	Late Miller II
5	1141	1180 ± 40	Middle Miller III
12	1142	1160 ± 45	Middle Miller III
Site 1Gr2			
56	1159	490 ± 50	Late Miller II
75	1160	970 ± 40	Middle Miller III
70	1161	880 ± 50	Middle Miller III
115	1162	760 ± 55	Early Miller IIIb
90	1163	1130 ± 45	Middle Miller III
66	1164	980 ± 40	Middle Miller III
126	1165	730 ± 50	Early Miller IIIb
97	1166	910 ± 55	Early Miller IIIb
Site 1Pi33			
51 (Zone B)	1231	1030 ± 55	Terminal Miller III
51 (Zone B)	1232	1030 ± 55	Terminal Miller III
6 (Structure 1)	1233	1410 ± 45	Moundville III

Note: Samples processed by Dicarb Radioisotope Company.

Plain var. *Turkey Paw* and Turkey Paw Fabric Marked var. *Gordo*. Turkey Paw Cord Marked var. *Moon Lake* and Turkey Paw Punctated var. *Turkey Paw* are sporadic and together constitute less than 2 percent of the ceramic complex (fig. 16) (Jenkins 1982, 87–89). The co-occurrence of bone, sand, and grog as tempers is problematic but may indicate a shift in clay source and an attempt to modify the aplastic clay body inclusions to account for poorly understood properties of a new clay. The limestone-tempered types when taken together form the late Middle Woodland Copena Complex in the Tennessee valley (Walthall 1973, 1979), and their occurrences in Turkey Paw contexts indicate contacts with that area.

The Turkey Paw subphase is dated by ceramic cross-finds, and radiometric determinations. Limestone-tempered Copena ceramics which occur consistently in Turkey Paw components were made between 100 B.C. and A.D. 500. Cross-finds of McLeod complex and Weeden Island types indicate an A.D. 400 to 500 time correspondence (Bullen 1966, Jenkins 1982, Wimberly 1960). The earliest radiometric determination on carbon from 1Pi61 gave an A.D. 420±170 estimate. A slightly later carbon date of 490±50 years was drawn from a 1Gr2 sample, and the latest date of A.D. 680±75 years was taken from charcoal at 1Gr1x1 (table 1) (Jenkins 1982, 96). It would therefore seem reasonable to estimate the Turkey Paw subphase at A.D. 400 to A.D. 600.

The Miller Three Phase

Material Culture

The Miller Three phase, although obviously developed from a Miller Two base, expresses a metastable rather than a dynamic equilibrium. For this reason we group it with the Deasonville phase, the McKelvey phase, and other lower Mississippi valley complexes as part of a Baytown Temporal variant. Miller Three ceramics are predominantly grog tempered. Sand-tempered and grog-tempered wares are found in roughly equal numbers early in the phase, but as the phase unfolds, the use of grog grows in popularity at the expense of sand. For example, early in Miller Three the sand-tempered Baldwin Plain var. *Blubber* comprises 30 to 40 percent of the ceramic complex and grog-tempered Baytown Plain var. *Roper* approximately 20 percent (fig. 20). Nearer the end of the Miller Three phase grog-tempered Mulberry Creek Cord Marked var. *Aliceville* constitutes from 65 to 70 percent of the ceramic inventory and Baytown Plain var. *Roper* another 10 to 14 percent. Shell-tempered wares, harbingers of things to come, appear in small amounts, 1 percent or less, at the very end of Miller Three times. Then, too, there is a growth in popularity of cord-marked surface treatment at the expense of the plain wares

Figure 20. Pottery of the Miller Three Phase: (A, B, C) Mulberry Creek Cord Marked;
(D) Gainesville Simple Stamped; (E, G, I) Alligator Incised; (F) Yeates Net Impressed;
(H) Evansville Punctated; (J, K, L) Baytown Plain

which characterized late Miller Two phase ceramics. Roughly 60 percent of the early Miller Three pottery types, more specifically Baldwin Plain var. *Blubber* and Baytown Plain vars. *Roper* and *Tishomingo,* are plain; 65 to 75 percent of the late types (primarily Mulberry Creek Cord Marked var. *Aliceville*) are cord marked. There are, as earlier, strong correlations between specific surface finishes and vessel forms. Baytown Plain vars. *Roper* and *Tishomingo* are associated with flat-bottomed beakers having gently outsloping sides. Unlike their earlier Miller Two counterparts, however, they lack heavy slablike bases and loop handles. Rounded base, plain surface bowls appear but less frequently than beakers. Cord-marked surfaces, like those of Mulberry Creek Cord Marked vars. *Aliceville* and *Tishomingo* appear on large, shallow, hemispherical bowls and deep hemispherical or conoidal containers. Fabric-marked surfaces of Withers Fabric Marked vars. *Gainesville* and *Craigs Landing* type appear on large hemispherical bowls as do the decorative treatments typical of the minority types: Alligator Incised vars. *Oxbow, Gainesville,* and *Geiger;* Avoyelles Punctated var. *Tubbs Creek;* Evansville Punctated var. *Tishabee;* Gainesville Cob Marked var. *El Rod;* and Gainesville Simple Stamped var. *Hickory* (fig. 20).

Miller Three lithic technology was characterized by: (1) the introduction of smaller, triangular projectile points; (2) a reduction in size of nontriangular (i.e., Miller Two) projectile point types; (3) the lack of cores as an integral part of manufacturing debris; (4) heat pretreatment hotter than in Miller Two times, which produced a deep red, rather than pink, product; and (5) an overall reduction in the size of flakes. The first appearance of small triangular projectile points is a diagnostic element in Miller Three lithic assemblages. Three varieties of small triangular points were manufactured: Madison var. *Gainesville,* Hamilton var. *Gainesville,* and Pickens Triangular var. *Pickens.* The Pickens point, var. *Pickens,* was most popular in early Miller Three. It measures more than 25 mm in length, which makes it the largest of the three triangular forms. These Pickens points, which are uniformly thin and well flaked, have straight bases and excurvate blade edges. Madison points, popular later, have straight-blade edges and a straight base. The Madison type, var. *Gainesville,* persisted through later Miller Three into Mississippian times. The Hamilton type, var. *Gainesville,* which has an incurvate base and blade edges, was more popular late in the Miller Three phase (Ensor 1981).

A reduction in the size of nontriangular points, the lack of cores in lithic detritus, and heat treating the raw material at a higher temperature were related. Miller Two phase peoples heat treated locally obtained yellow cherts at relatively low temperatures. They thus produced a dull pinkish red raw material, inhibited thermal explosion, and provided large spalls and cobbles from which cores, large-stemmed points, and flaked tools could be made. Miller Three stonesmiths heated their raw material at higher temperatures. This change produced large numbers of small bright red flakes and fire-cracked chert but did not produce enough large pieces for the frequent manufacture of cores, large-stemmed points, and large flake tools. In effect, Miller Three stonesmiths selected the raw material for their projectile points and flake tools from smaller, more intensely heat-treated spalls than their Miller Two ancestors had done, in the process casting aside the remaining fire-cracked chert which became a diagnostic feature of Miller Three phase middens. Utilized flakes and spalls are relatively common in Miller Three phase remains as are bifaces, knives, blanks, preforms, perforators, and choppers. Ground stone tools are relatively rare, consisting of hammerstones, abraders, pitted stones (nutting stones), anvil stones, and mullers (Ensor 1981).

Subsistence Practices

Subsistence data from the area of Gainesville Lake indicate that nut foods were of major import to the diet of Miller Three phase populations. Hickory nuts and acorns were most common, indicating, we presume, a continuing reliance upon them as a major food source. Maize was added to the inventory of plant foods in Miller Three times, but the frequency of corn remains, if indicative of frequency of use, suggests that it was not a major carbohydrate source (table 2). Corn accounted for less than 1 percent of the floral remains at all Miller Three components but did seem to occur more frequently in late rather than early Miller Three contexts, indicating, we suppose, a growth in dependence upon it. Relatively large numbers of seeds from "wild" plants were also present, among them wild bean (*Strophostyles* sp.); beggar's-lice (*Desmodium* sp.); blackberry, or dewberry (*Rubus* sp.); panic grass (*Panicum* sp.); and maypop (*Passiflora incarnata*). Many seeds of weedy annuals such as goosefoot, pokeweed, pigweed, wood sorrel, knotweed, and chickweed were probably a consequence of the clearing which accompanied base-camp residence (Caddell 1981a).

Significant trends can be seen in the Miller Three phase faunal data. The number of deer taken, calculated by bone weight per component, declined. In early Miller Three components, deer bone constituted 88 percent of the vertebrates. Later, deer bone dropped to a mean of 76.5 percent and reached a low of 70.9 percent near the end of Miller Three times (fig. 19, A). While deer declined, the number of small mammals and reptiles increased as did the use of shellfish (fig. 19, B). In early Miller Three components turtle, bird, and fish remains represented, respectively, 6.6 percent, 1.8 percent, and 0.9 percent of the bone sample (Woodrick 1981, table 37). Rabbit (7.3 percent), opossum (5.1 percent), turkey (4.1 percent), gray fox (1.8 percent), raccoon (1.7 percent), beaver (1.4 percent), and squirrel (1.2 percent) constituted the most

Table 2. *Summary of Plant Food Remains from Miller III and Summerville I Features*

	No. of Features	Percentage of Total Weight					
		Hickory	Acorn	Walnut	Zea	Wood	Other
Summerville I[a]							
Lubbub Creek	7	1.28	0.64	—	51.44	37.66	8.97
Cofferdam[a]							
Lubbub Creek	37	30.18	9.11	0.27	0.12	52.28	8.04
1Gr1x1[b]	8	8.28	1.64	0.05	p	39.61	50.12
1Gr2[b]	10	12.47	0.80	—	p	54.14	32.60
Catfish Bend-							
Gainesville[b] 1Pi61	16	31.69	ss	0.60	ss	58.15	9.56
Vienna[b]	10	39.02	0.64	1.27	—	57.07	2.00

Note: Dashes = no data available; p = present, weight negligible; ss = recovered from soil samples but not from ¼-in. screen.
[a]Flotation samples from features.
[b]¼-in. screen.
Sources: Caddell 1981b, tables 4 and 6; Caddell 1981a, tables 9, 13, and 20.

important small mammals. Late in the phase, the mean bone weight of turtles was 16.1 percent and of fish, 4.1 percent, roughly double its earlier value. The mean weight of bird bone dropped to 4.2 percent, that of opossum to 4.7 percent, and beaver to 1.0 percent, but the percentage used of other small mammals increased markedly: rabbit to 8.6 percent, squirrel to 11.6 percent, and raccoon to 8.3 percent. Turkey bone also increased from 4.1 to 6.0 percent by weight from early to late Miller Three (Woodrick 1981, table 38) (fig. 18, A). The density of shellfish remains increased from an early mean of 1,063 grams per cubic foot of debris to a late mean of 1,235 grams per cubic foot of debris (fig. 18, B). All in all, there seems to have been a gradual shift from first-line faunal resources like deer to second-line resources like rabbit, squirrel, raccoon, fish, turtle, and shellfish.

Settlement Pattern

During the Miller Three phase, oval, dome-shaped dwellings built of poles covered with grass, bark, and/or hides were replaced by rectangular houses with pole and thatch walls constructed in shallow house pits and presumably covered with a steeply pitched thatched roof. Some oval houses, transitional forms perhaps, were also built in shallow pits and both kinds of houses were provided with centrally located basin-shaped hearths. The remains of four oval and four rectangular houses have been explored (fig. 13). Two of the four oval houses were found at the Tibbee Creek site (O'Hear et al. 1981). Both of them were constructed of individually set posts. One was 5 m (16.40 ft.) at its longest axis, and about its perimeter it had sixty-five wall posts with a mean post diameter of 18.30 cm (7.20 in.). The disposition of eleven of twenty-five intermural posts led O'Hear to interpret them as the remains of an internal partition. A charcoal sample from this structure's central hearth yielded a radiocarbon determination of 965±55 (O'Hear et al. 1981, 99–105). The other oval house had been partially destroyed. An arc of thirty postholes indicating individually set posts with a mean of 18 cm (7.09 in.) was all that remained. A third Miller Three oval house was found at the Bynum site (Cotter and Corbett 1951). It had forty-four individually set posts which formed an oval 4.75 m (15 ft.) long at its longest axis and a centrally located, basin-shaped hearth. The fourth and final oval house was found at 1Pi61. It was 3.35 m (11 ft.) in maximum axis length and had a basin-shaped subterranean floor 21.34 cm (0.7 ft.) deep. An elongate basin-shaped depression (3.5 m, or 10 ft. long) lying at a right angle to this structure's southern edge may have served as an entrance. Two tightly flexed corpses had been interred beneath its floor (Jenkins and Ensor 1981). The four rectangular houses, all of them built in terminal Miller Three times, were also found at 1Pi61. Although not deep (a maximum of 0.4 ft.), all four had been built in and over excavated house pits. To form walls small posts had been set close together immediately inside the edge of each semisubterranean floor (fig. 21). One of the houses, which also had its wall posts set in trenches, had been rebuilt since both wall trenches along its longest sides cut through previously set individual posts. The same house had a burial beneath its floor. The smaller of the four houses was 10 by 6 feet; the largest, 15 by 11 feet; and three of the four had central hearths.

The Miller Three economy has been characterized as the ultimate in floodplain/forest efficiency (Jenkins 1982, 78). There seems to have been a dramatic population growth and an increase in sedentary life. The growth in population has been inferred from the greater number and size of Miller Three sedentary settlements and transitory camps; the increase in sedentary life, from the larger and denser middens that accompanied them. Miller Three floodplain settlements, for example, invariably contain compact dark middens with sizable amounts of shell, animal bone, pottery, fire-cracked rock, charcoal, and other detritus, quite clearly the offal of sedentary life. Transitory camps contain far less in the way of midden deposits. They consist of sparse ceramic and lithic scatters interspersed with limited amounts of offal. Some of these small sites do, however, contain large amounts of lithic debris, leading to the conjecture that they were hunting camps. The large Miller Three seden-

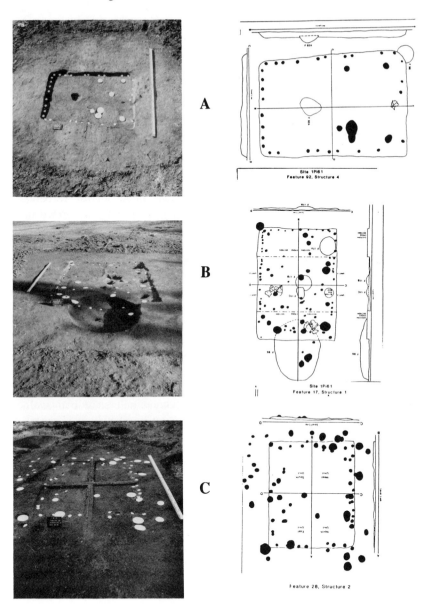

Figure 21. Miller Three House Remains at 1Pi61

tary settlements (base camps) were concentrated in the floodplain flanking the
Tombigbee and were most numerous in an area extending from immediately
north of Columbus, Mississippi, south to Demopolis, Alabama—a region
roughly coterminus with the Black Prairie physiographic district. Transitory
camps were located in the fall line hills to the east of the floodplains. To the
west, transitory camps were found in the Black Prairie (fig. 12). The larger,
and more permanent, floodplain settlements, like their Miller Two prototypes,
were occupied in the spring, summer, and fall (see Jenkins 1981, 77–91); the
transitory camps were the consequence of a winter pattern of small group
hunting and foraging.

In sum, the economic evidence from Miller Three sites suggests larger,
more sedentary populations; an increase in the use of second-line resources;
and the addition of maize as a cultigen, albeit in limited amounts. The interaction of these three variables may be conceptualized, we suggest, as a syn-
drome in which population growth and the concomitant stress on first-line
food resources triggered greater dependence upon second-line resources and
upon tended or cultivated plants, which in turn stimulated an increase in the
commitment to sedentary life and more population growth, which triggered
even greater dependence upon second-line resources and cultigens, and so on.

Ceremonialism

Miller Three mortuary ritual was a mere shadow of what had gone before.
There were no elaborate stage settings, no crematoria, no crematory altars, no
charnel houses, and no mounds. Flesh burial in simple pits was now the rule
(fig. 13), and, on occasion, the burial chamber was not dug specifically for the
corpse. Sometimes recycled storage pits were used as burial crypts (fig. 22,
D). There was a transformation in terminal Miller Three times from flexed
inhumations in circular or oval pits (fig. 22, A, C) to extended or semiex-
tended burial in rectangular graves (fig. 22, B). Within a village the dead were
placed in dug chambers; in recycled storage pits; beneath house floors; and in
special tracts, or cemeteries (fig. 22). Burial goods (e.g., greenstone celts,
pottery, shell beads, shell pendants, and bears' teeth) occurred sporadically in
early Miller Three burials but became a more consistent component of later
interments. Burial inclusions occurred with males and females, adults and
children. There was no discernible bias for more frequent inclusions with any
single age or sex, hence burial goods do not seem to be markers of the status
and prestige earned or acquired by the deceased (Jenkins 1982, 77–91). This
does not mean, of course, that burial inclusions could not have been tokens of
the status-striving efforts of living relatives. Ambitious relatives of the deceased may, for instance, have promoted their interests through wealth manip-

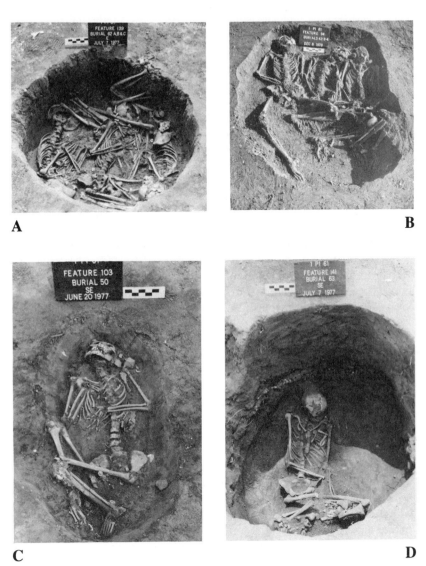

Figure 22. Miller Three Interments at 1Pi61

ulation, distribution, and destruction at important social and religious events. In such cases the destruction (i.e., removal) of wealth through its inclusion in a burial would be but one instance of a broader pattern of status striving.

Archaeological surveys of the upper Tombigbee (Atkinson 1978, Blakeman 1976, Hubbert 1978, Penman 1977) indicate that the northern range of Miller Three occupation overlapped that of Miller Two but was by no means coextensive with it. Most of the Miller Three sites in this northern range are also much smaller than their counterparts to the south, giving them a frontierlike appearance. Recent surveys along the central and lower Tombigbee indicate that sedentary Miller Three settlements did not occur south of Demopolis, Alabama (Brose, Jenkins, and Weisman 1982). Smaller, transitory camps are found 10 to 15 miles farther south, but these lie on the extreme southern edge of occupation. Thus, it now seems that despite marked population growth from Miller Two to Miller Three times, there was a substantial contraction in the amount of riverbottom territory occupied—a contraction of from 15 to 30 river miles. To the east the Miller Three and West Jefferson phase distributions overlap in the Black Warrior valley 10 miles north of its junction with the Tombigbee (Jenkins and Nielsen 1974). The greater frequency of cord-marked pottery in West Jefferson components south of Moundville seems, for example, to have been a consequence of their proximity to Miller Three populations in the lower Warrior valley (Welch 1980, fig. 3). The western distribution of Miller Three peoples has not yet been well defined (fig. 12). We suspect, however, that it overlaps with at least one of the Baytown variant phases in the lower Mississippi valley (see Penman 1977; Phillips 1970, 907).

Chronology and Subphases

The temporal span of the Miller Three phase has been conservatively estimated at A.D. 600 to 1100. The evidence for this estimate consists of twenty-one radiometric determinations run on charcoal from six components. The radiometric assays yielded the following distribution of determinations by century: one late in the sixth century (A.D. 570±395), six in the eighth century, one in the ninth century, four in the tenth century, three in the eleventh century, four in the twelfth century, one in the thirteenth century (A.D. 1215±110), and one in the fifteenth century (A.D. 1465±70). The large standard deviation for the sixth- and thirteenth-century determinations indicates a lack of good agreement between separate sample counts and leads us to treat the results cautiously. The fifteenth-century determination is considered suspect by virtue of its lack of fit with the others (table 1). Ceramic cross-finds from radiocarbon-dated complexes in the Mississippi and Tennessee valleys also indicate a seventh- to twelfth-century placement for Miller Three (see Jenkins 1982, 82).

Jenkins (1982, 69–73) uses ceramic evidence to divide the Miller Three phase into four subphases: Vienna, Catfish Bend, Cofferdam, and Gainesville. The wares produced by Vienna subphase potters were sand or grog tempered with plain or cord-marked surfaces. Sand was the predominant temper early in the subphase; grog, the most popular aplastic later. In early Vienna complexes, Baldwin Plain var. *Blubber* occurs in frequencies of 30 to 40 percent; Baytown Plain var. *Roper,* in frequencies of 20 percent; Baytown Plain var. *Tishomingo,* in frequencies of 12 to 15 percent; and Furrs Cord Marked var. *Pickens,* in frequencies of 10 percent. Mulberry Creek Cord Marked var. *Tishomingo* occurs in a frequency of 1 percent or less. Other minority types include Withers Fabric Marked var. *Gainesville* (2 percent or less), Withers Fabric Marked var. *River Bend* (1 percent or less), Alligator Incised vars. *Oxbow* and *Gainesville* (less than 0.50 percent). Trade pieces include sherds broken from pots of Weeden Island Red Filmed var. *unspecified,* Keith Incised var. *unspecified,* Porter Zoned Incised var. *unspecified,* McLeod Check Stamped and Simple Stamped types. In late Vienna subphase complexes, Baytown Plain var. *Roper* ranges from 45 to 55 percent of the ceramic inventory, Baytown Plain var. *Tishomingo* declines to less than 2 percent, Mulberry Creek Cord Marked var. *Aliceville* increases to 25 percent, Mulberry Creek Cord Marked var. *Tishomingo* remains at a frequency of 1 percent, but Withers Fabric Marked var. *Gainesville* doubles in popularity to capture a 5 percent share of the ceramic inventory. Minority types which appear for the first time late in the Vienna subphase include Yeates Net Impressed (fig. 20) var. *Yeates,* Gainesville Simple Stamped var. *Hickory,* Solomon Brushed var. *Fairfield,* Evansville Punctated var. *Tishabee,* Lareto Red Filmed var. *unspecified.* Alligator Incised vars. *Oxbow* and *Gainesville* continue at less than 0.50 percent (fig. 16) (Jenkins 1982, 69–73).

By the Catfish Bend subphase the popularity of plain grog-tempered pottery had decreased, the popularity of grog-tempered cord-marked pottery had increased, and sand was infrequently used as a temper. For example, the relative amounts of Baytown Plain var. *Roper* decrease and those of Mulberry Creek Cord Marked var. *Aliceville* increase. Withers Fabric Marked var. *Gainesville* also increases. All of the grog-tempered minority types present during the Vienna subphase continue into the Catfish Bend subphase and several new varieties make their first appearance. Among the latter are Alligator Incised var. *Geiger,* Gainesville Cob Marked var. *Elrod,* and Avoyelles Punctated var. *Tubbs Creek,* Alligator Incised var. *Oxbow,* and Withers Fabric Marked var. *Gainesville.* Taken collectively, however, the minority wares account for less than 3 percent of the ceramic complex (fig. 16) (Jenkins 1982, 69–73).

Cofferdam components contain a two- or three-to-one dominance of Mulberry Creek Cord Marked var. *Aliceville* over Baytown Plain var. *Roper.* During the earliest part of the Cofferdam subphase, Mulberry Creek Cord Marked var. *Aliceville* constitutes 55 to 60 percent, and Baytown Plain var. *Roper,* 20 to 30 percent of the ceramic inventory. By the end of the subphase, Mulberry Creek Cord Marked var. *Aliceville* comprises 65 to 70 percent and Baytown Plain 15 percent or less of the ceramic complex. Through the same span of time the amount of Withers Fabric Marked var. *Gainesville* decreases to 7 percent. Minority ceramics of the Cofferdam subphase include Alligator Incised var. *Oxbow* and var. *Yeates,* Gainesville Simple Stamped var. *Hickory,* Solomon Brushed var. *Fairfield,* and Evansville Punctated var. *Tishabee.* Several shell-tempered sherds have been found in Cofferdam components reflecting contact with Mississippians (fig. 16) (Jenkins 1982, 69–73).

The ceramic wares produced by Gainesville subphase potters, for the most part, closely resemble those of their Catfish Bend precursors. The types and varieties of grog-tempered ceramics found in components of Catfish Bend and Gainesville subphases are practically identical. There are, however, two very important differences. The Baytown Plain var. *Roper* vessels of the Gainesville subphase sometimes carry grog-tempered loop handles which are probably copies of contemporaneous Mississippian counterparts. Morphologically identical grog- and shell-tempered loop handles were, for instance, found in the same feature at the Gainesville subphase component of 1Pi33. The most distinctive ceramic element of the Gainesville subphase is, however, the occurrence of shell-tempered wares as minority types and the appearance of shell- and grog-tempered pottery, albeit in a frequency of less than 0.50 percent. A few Gainesville potters seem to have cautiously adopted Mississippian practices (Jenkins 1982, 69–73).

To recapitulate and synthesize, Vienna (A.D. 600 to 800) and Catfish Bend (A.D. 900 to 1000) are temporally sequent subphases of the Miller Three phase. Cofferdam (A.D. 900 to 1200) and Gainesville (A.D. 1000 to 1100) are roughly contemporaneous but materially and areally distinct Miller Three subphases which follow the Catfish Bend subphase. The major difference between the people who produced the Cofferdam and those who created the Gainesville remains lies in the former's resistance to Mississippian ideas and the latter's willingness to incorporate them. The Gainesville population's move toward Mississippian norms occurred in the densely occupied Miller Three heartland. It affected pottery making (the manufacture of shell-tempered or shell- and grog-tempered pottery and shell-tempered or shell- and grog-tempered loop handles), stone tool manufacture (the production of the Madison var. *Gainesville* point), house type (the construction of semisubterranean rectangular houses with pole and thatch walls having a peaked thatched roof), burial customs (semiflexed and extended burial in rectangular graves grouped into plots or cemeteries, and subsistence (the cultivation of increasing amounts of maize). The Cofferdam resistance to Mississippianization resulted in a clear continuity between the ceramic (grog- and sand-tempered cord-marked wares), lithic (Hamilton var. *Gainesville* points), housebuilding (oval, dome-shaped timber structures covered with grass, bark, or hide), and burial practices (flexed bodies in oval or circular pits) of Catfish Bend and later peoples.

4. The Mississippian Stage

By A.D. 1000, Mississippian peoples who resided in substantial communities and built impressive fortifications and earthen monuments were found throughout the Southeast (Griffin 1967, Jennings 1974, Walthall 1980, Willey 1966). Mississippian culture appeared first in the central Mississippi valley south of St. Louis sometime after the ninth century. From here it spread to three distinct but related centers: Cahokia in the central Mississippi valley; the Caddoan area of eastern Oklahoma, Texas, and Louisiana with its major center at Spiro; and the Tennessee-Cumberland drainage with major centers at Etowah and Moundville (Walthall 1980, 185). Mississippians achieved relatively dense populations capable of harnessing impressive amounts of human energy. The use of human and natural resources was organized through and directed by chiefs who controlled the distribution of maize and other crops grown on the region's self-fertilizing alluvial soils (Walthall 1980, 192–93). Chiefs and other functionaries commanded the goods and services of widespread farming populations, directed the construction of monumental public works, regulated the conduct of war and trade, monitored the production of those specially crafted goods which carried elements of an esoteric iconography, and encouraged the growth and conduct of a symbol-rich and elaborate ceremonialism (see Peebles 1974, 1978; Peebles and Kus 1977; and Walthall 1980, 196–245).

Mississippian leaders treated with other groups to facilitate trade and acquire scarce commodities (salt, greenstone, or copper, for example) or resorted to war to achieve their ends. War or the threat of war was a regular feature of Mississippian life if we are to judge by the elaborate fortifications thrown up about major centers. These included ditches or dry moats backed with earthen embankments and wooden palisades with bastions set at enfilade. Then, too, there were fortified, bastion-protected gates approached by narrow, winding entrances which allowed only a single man to pass at a time, his progress slowed by several turns before access to the interior was assured (see Lafferty 1973). Considerable effort was required to raise and maintain these extensive defenses, and in time the materials for rebuilding and repair would have to be transported from farther and farther away. Hence, the social and material costs of sustaining a major center's defenses would escalate with each generation and each rebuilding. Larson (1972, 383–92) has argued that these were necessary costs, for the objective of war was seizure of the self-fertilizing farmlands which the Mississippian economy and chiefly prestige required.

Mississippian builders also expended considerable time and energy in the construction of platform mounds (fig. 23). In fact, they produced the largest earthen structures in North America prior to the construction of the Missouri River dams in the 1950s. Each mound sloped inward from base to summit, and at least one side usually carried a ramp or staircase that provided access from ground level to platform top. Some mounds carried at least one perishable summit-top temple or dwelling, and although the available evidence is limited, we have every reason to expect one or more richly stocked burial and a succession of prior "temples/dwellings" within them (see Walthall 1980, 196–245). These earth-filled temple-tombs presumably signaled a form of ancestor veneration which was intimately related to a system of ranking and the means of status and prestige distribution. The mounds were frequently built in major and minor stages with new, thick or thin layers of soil added at appropriate intervals. Thus, mound construction was periodic, but even so, considerable labor was expended during most construction episodes and in the maintenance of any given stage as well (see Knight 1981).

Horizon

Iconographic representations were an integral part of Mississippian ceremonialism. They played an important role in burial ritual to judge by their presence in the graves of some members of the society, presumably an elite of one kind or another. Some at least were warriors whose social standing was signaled by ritual weapons and symbols of war. According to Brown (1976, 115–36), burial goods indicative of war included ceremonial maces, celts, monolithic axes, long knives or swords of delicately chipped flint, and bilobed arrows rendered in the form of copper cutouts and engraved shell or embossed copper plate renditions of the falcon and falcon impersonator. As impressive as the list of war-related symbols may be, Mississippian iconogra-

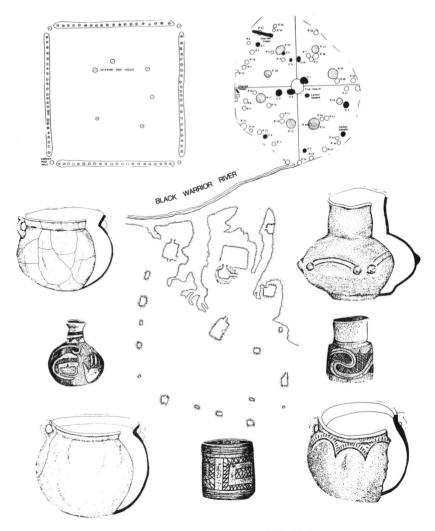

Figure 23. Artifacts and Features of the Moundville Variant

phy was not restricted to glorifying military exploits. Iconographic elements like the cross (including the Greek cross and swastika), sun circles, bilobed arrows, forked eye, barred oval, hand and eye, skull, femur, radius, and ulna, and naturalistic or stylized representations of animal or animal impersonators were applied to ceramics, shell, stone, bone, wood, and cold-worked copper artifacts whose possession and use was by no means confined to males, let alone warriors (Griffin 1967, 190). The rapid spread of this Mississippian iconography and the high redundancy it exhibited through its range suggests the existence of a cult or group of cults, a horizon which integrated far-flung Mississippian communities. Thus, Waring and Holder's original conclusions are still cogent:

> There existed in the prehistoric southeast a highly developed cult or cult complex, integrated with and fundamentally dependent upon a horticultural base. This cult was synthesized within the southeastern United States in a single community or restricted group of communities at a relatively late date from elements introduced from Middle America. This integration probably took place in the Middle Mississippi Basin. From this center the cult spread rapidly crossing tribal boundaries, flowered abruptly and passed almost as quickly reaching historic levels only in attenuated form. [Waring and Holder 1945, 32]

As rich and full as it may seem to the archaeologist, when put in worldwide perspective, the Mississippian resembles many other preindustrial farming societies. People were assured a life of hard work at high risk of death or disability from disease, accident, or combat. Women had frequent pregnancies and lost many children in infancy. Children assumed the obligations of adult labor at a relatively early age. Life was usually short, lived within a restricted geographic range, and spent in the company of a small number of one's fellows and kinsmen. Education and experience were limited to the exigencies of daily life. Noble and commoner alike shared a similar menu (cf. Schoeninger and Peebles 1980), and both built and lived in one-room huts. For commoners, there was a continual round of field clearing, harvesting, tool and implement manufacture, palisade construction and maintenance, and mound building interrupted periodically by the physical exhilaration of combat or the spiritual excitement of ceremony. For the nobility there were plans to make, managerial details to check, and ritual matters to attend to as well. Both commoner and noble, however, participated, if differentially so, in the prestige associated with prehistoric North America's most influential social, political, and economic power (see Walthall 1980, 189–96).

Periods

The Mississippian stage may be divided into Early (A.D. 1000 to 1250), Middle (A.D. 1250 to 1400), and Late (A.D. 1400 to 1540) periods (Jenkins 1982, 187–89). The Early period was marked by the spread of a Mississippian lifestyle to far-flung regions of the Southeast. That intensive food production was an integral part of Mississippian life from its inception to its fall is indisputable. Nevertheless, the process by which crop growing was spread throughout the region is a matter of great interest and some debate. There are three contrastive views: (1) about A.D. 1000, immigrant Mississippian farming populations displaced resident Woodland groups (Caldwell 1958, 64); (2) from A.D. 700 to A.D. 900, resident Woodland hunting and gathering groups were transformed (i.e., Mississippianized) through the diffusion of ideas and practices typical of crop-growing peoples in other regions (Griffin 1985); and (3) from A.D. 800 to 1000 a limited influx of cultivators introduced ideas and practices which transformed resident hunters and harvesters and stimulated a fusion of resident with immigrant to produce local versions of a Mississippian lifestyle (Jenkins 1976). Any one of the three explanations may apply in a given locality; that is, the area could have been occupied via large-scale immigration, it could have been the scene of minimal immigrations accompanied by the incorporation of resident groups, or it could have been the geographic space in which resident groups were transformed through diffusion of ideas and practices from elsewhere. All three could not, however, have applied to the same area simultaneously, nor could any two. Each case must, of course, be considered on its own merits as judged by appropriate forms of archaeological inquiry (Faulkner 1971).

The Middle period (A.D. 1250–1400) witnessed the consolidation, internal growth, and elaboration of a Mississippian way of life. A three-part settlement system featuring large multimound centers; smaller, single-mound satellite villages; and scattered farming hamlets and homesteads emerged (Peebles 1978, Peebles and Kus 1977, Steponaitis 1978). Fortifications around major centers were elaborated; the practice of mound building, rebuilding, and purificatory enlargement reached its apogee; and southern cult symbolism achieved its most elaborate and intensely integrated form. Long-distance trade produced its greatest volume (skimpy as it was when compared with that of Mexico or South America) and was accompanied by part-time craft specialization in the production of a limited range of luxury goods, namely those with a value that was primarily symbolic rather than utilitarian (see Hardin 1980, Walthall 1980). In many areas, populations grew to their all-time pre-Columbian peak, and the floodplain agriculture practiced by Mississippians reached its maximal extent. In sum, the years between A.D. 1250 and A.D. 1400 witnessed the peak expression of "Mississippian civilization." Shortly thereafter, during the Late period (A.D. 1400–1540), the Mississippian populations of the Southeast experienced those modifications of lifestyle and distribution that archaeologists identify as a cultural decline. The intensity of mound building began to subside, concentrated populations began to disperse, elaborate fortifications were not regularly maintained, and the integrative force of southern cult symbolism waned, as, we presume, did the strength of traditionally defined authority (Sheldon 1974).

Variant

The areal manifestation of the Mississippian stage in west-central Alabama is the Moundville variant. At least three, possibly more, local expressions of this variant can be found in the major river drainages of western
Alabama and eastern Mississippi. Peebles and Blitz's (1981) Summerville I–

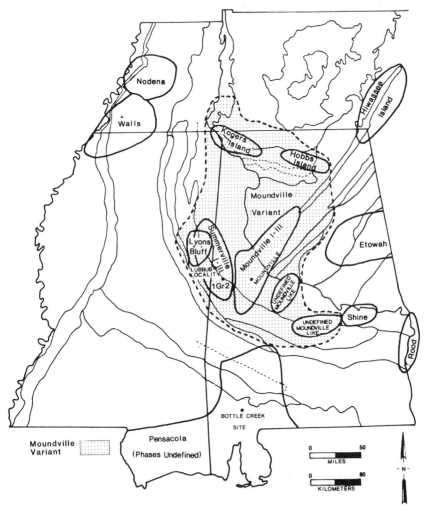

Figure 24. Selected Mississippian Sites and Manifestations

III continuum in the Lubbub Creek locality is a local manifestation of the
variant in the central Tombigbee drainage. Marshall's (1977, 53–58) Tibbee
Creek–Lyons Bluff sequence 45 miles to the northwest is another. Steponaitis's (1978) Moundville I–III sequence for the large center and its satellites on the Black Warrior River is a third (fig. 24). The Moundville, Tibbee
Creek, and Summerville manifestations are so very closely related in time,
space, and content that it would be difficult at best to disentangle the events
which gave them their own trajectories to change. We group the three sequences into a single Moundville variant to emphasize their relatedness. In
doing so, we presume that the sequence of phases defined for each will express the separate trajectories that distinguish them, despite the difficulties of
disentangling the intertwined events and processes that we presume created
each in the image of the others.

Tradition

The tradition which ran through and hence integrated the separable phases
of the Moundville variant had, at its core, the manufacture of both coarse and
fine shell-tempered ceramics. The coarse ware contained shell inclusions
greater than 1.5 mm in diameter, was usually unburnished, and was fired in an
oxydizing environment that produced a finish that varied from pale yellow to
deep brown. The fine ware contained very fine shell particles (well below 1.5
mm in diameter), was usually thoroughly burnished, and was frequently fired
in a reducing atmosphere. To produce burnished surfaces, the prehistoric ar-
tisan wet the vessel to float the finer particles then rubbed back and forth
briskly with a smooth stone. Later when such surfaces were burned in an
oxygen-deficient atmosphere, they turned black, producing a visual effect
which resembled a film (Steponaitis 1978). Both coarse and fine wares were
built by a method most clearly described as mold-assisted coiling in which
mold-made sections were fastened to coiled sections, coiled sections were
fastened to one another, or molds were used to support and turn coil-made
sections during production (van der Leeuw 1980). The predominant coarse-
ware vessel shape was a globular bodied round-shouldered jar with either an
abruptly constricted neck and an outflaring rim, or a gently constricted neck
and an outflaring rim. Fine wares occurred in flaring rim bowls and sub-
globular bottles with pedestal bases (fig. 23) (Steponaitis 1978). Both fine and
coarse shell-tempered ceramics co-occurred with small (less than 25 mm
long), straight-based, straight-sided projectile points; evidence for crop growing; the hunting of deer and smaller game for meat and hides; the use of
aboveground storage facilities; and square or rectangular mud plaster, pole,
and thatch houses (fig. 23) (Jenkins 1982, 142–47).

In short, the Mississippian stage caps the three-stage quasi series in the Tombigbee drainage. Like its Gulf Formational and Woodland predecessors, it can be divided into three sequent periods. The earliest of these (A.D. 1000 to 1250) is marked by the advent of crop growing and the formulation of an esoteric body of ritual which legitimized differences in social standing and justified the construction of monumental public works. During the intermediate period (A.D. 1250 to 1400) monumental public works (mound and palisade building), ceremonialism, trade, craft specialization, population growth, and the extension of floodplain horticulture all reached their apogee. The terminal period (A.D. 1400 to 1540) is marked by a decline—a modification of lifestyle and population distribution that began slowly but ultimately affected the scale of public works, the number and size of local population aggregates, and by extension, those forms of ritual and political life that depended upon a concentrated populace. All three periods host phases of a single spatially distinct variation of the Mississippian theme—the Moundville variant. Moundville variant remains were created by peoples who, like others in the Southeast, were using the iconographic elements of the southern cult. It was, in fact, the southern cult that spread rapidly through the region to form the horizon which integrates geographically distinct and widely separated phases of Mississippian culture. The temporally sequent phases of Mississippian culture are in turn integrated by the unfolding of a manufacturing tradition which had at its core the production of fine and coarse shell-tempered ceramics.

The Summerville One Phase

Material Culture

Summerville One phase peoples produced the first Moundville variant remains in the Tombigbee drainage during the Early period of the Mississippian stage. All Summerville ceramics were tempered with shell, but some contained additional inclusions of grog. Both coarse and fine shell-tempered wares were produced. The former (coarse wares) are represented by Mississippi Plain var. *Warrior,* Moundville Incised vars. *Moundville, Snows Bend,* and *Carrollton,* and Parkin Punctated var. *unspecified.* The latter (fine wares) included Bell Plain vars. *Hale* and *Big Sandy,* Moundville Engraved vars. *Hale* and *Big Sandy,* Moundville Engraved vars. *Fosters, Taylorville, Wiggins,* and *Tuscaloosa,* and Carthage Incised vars. *Moon Lake* and *Summerville* (Jenkins 1982, 124). Over 90 percent of the Summerville One ceramics had a plain surface. Mississippi Plain var. *Warrior,* for instance, comprised 80 to 85 percent of the inventory, Bell Plain var. *Hale* another 8 to 10 percent. Moundville Incised var. *Moundville* was the dominant decorated

type, followed in popularity by var. *Carrollton*. The fine wares, Carthage
Incised vars. *Moon Lake* and *Summerville* and Moundville Engraved var.
Tuscaloosa, were scarcely represented (Jenkins 1982, 124–25).

The inventory of nonceramic artifacts was rich and varied. Projectile points
of the Madison type and Gainesville variety were chipped by Summerville
One stonesmiths as were knives, scrapers, drills, and ceremonial flints (Ensor
1981, 39–40, 89–91). Stone was also pecked and ground into mortars, pes-
tles, manos, adzes, celts, axes, and bone tool sharpeners. Bone tools included
awls, needles, pins, drifts, and fish hooks. Shell was used for gorgets, dippers, bowls, masks, and hoe blades. Digging sticks, canoes, bows, arrow
shafts, bowls, and hafts of various kinds were made of wood; baskets, mats,
fish traps, and fans were made of woven cane. Fabrics were made of other
fibrous materials (plant fibers, hair, and/or feathers), woven without the aid of
the true loom, and copper was cold hammered into sheets which were embossed or cut into various shapes, sizes, and designs (see Walthall 1980, 187–
92).

Subsistence Practices

Like most Moundville variant settlements, those of Summerville One phase
peoples flanked the sinuous meander belts of a major river, in this case the
Tombigbee. Thus, farmsteads, villages, and ceremonial centers lay within
easy reach of sandy, well-drained, easy-to-work natural levee soils which had
the advantage of floodwater-borne nutrient enrichment. Summerville farmers
grew crops of maize, beans, squash, gourds, and other cultigens in the Lubbub Creek locality. Horticultural produce was supplemented with backwater
species of fish, migratory waterfowl, white-tailed deer, raccoon, rabbit, squirrel, turkey, hickory nuts, walnuts, acorns, persimmons, pawpaw, cherries,
plums, blackberries, and seed-bearing "pioneer" plants (see Scott 1981, 339–
42; Smith 1978, 1985). Thus, the greatest difference in plant use between
Miller Three and Summerville One populations did not lie in the species utilized, but in the marked difference in dependence upon cultigens—about 93
percent cultivated to 7 percent noncultivated foods for Summerville One peoples, contrasted with 1 to 3 percent cultigens to 97 percent wild foods for
Miller Three groups (table 2). Then, too, in Summerville One times, there
was a shift from dependence upon animals favoring a floodplain forest habitat
to those preferring an open or forest-edge environment; the shift was most
probably a consequence of floodplain deforestation which accompanied the
intensification of crop growing (Scott 1981, 363–64). In sum, Summerville
One peoples destroyed the vegetation growing on natural levee soils to plant

cultigens and in the process created a habitat for forest-edge animal species which they used as periodically rich and dependable sources of meat and skins. In addition, nonhorticultural plant foods were selected from the varieties of edible species favoring the habitats created by this juxtaposition of natural levee soils and forest-edge environments (see Caddell 1981a, 13–20; Smith 1985).

Settlement Pattern

The best examples of Summerville One phase houses and public buildings are found in the Lubbub Creek archaeological locality (Peebles and Blitz 1981). Excavations here revealed a village containing house remains and a mound precinct having the ruins of public buildings within it (fig. 25, C). Both were protected by a palisade which sealed off the interfluvial side of a U-shaped projection of land created by a bend in the Tombigbee River (Cole and Albright 1981) (fig. 25, D). Two oval house ruins and the remains of a possible outbuilding were excavated in the village proper. One of the oval houses had a long axis of 7 m (23 ft.), and the other a long axis of 6.5 m (21 ft.). The walls of both houses had been built of closely set posts held upright by individually dug holes. The upright wall posts were interlaced with horizontal split-cane lathing which was covered inside and out with a layer of mud plaster. A peaked thatched roof presumably covered each dwelling, and each contained a basin-shaped central hearth, one of which was constructed of puddled clay and had a raised rim 3 cm high. A radiocarbon assay on charcoal from one structure yielded a determination of A.D. 1050±55; a similar assay on the other yielded a date of A.D. 887±(?). The remains interpreted as an "outbuilding" lay 2 m from one of the dwellings and consisted of a square of postholes which were covered with a sheet of clay plaster (Peebles and Blitz 1981, 298).

The ruins of six public buildings lay beneath, hence obviously preceded, the construction of the Summerville mound at Lubbub Creek. The earliest building was constructed of individually set wall posts enclosing a circular area 3.5 m (11.5 ft.) in diameter. It yielded a radiocarbon date of 1080±90. The five other buildings in the mound precinct were either square or rectangular. The earliest of these was rectangular, with walls of individually set upright posts enclosing a prepared fired clay floor 5 to 10 cm (1.95 to 3.9 in.) thick, 6.5 m (21 ft.) long, and 4 m (13 ft.) wide. The last four buildings were paired. The earliest two had walls of closely spaced upright posts set in wall trenches—the only buildings at the site so constructed. One of these was 8 m square, had nonconvergent wall trenches and a centrally located basin-shaped

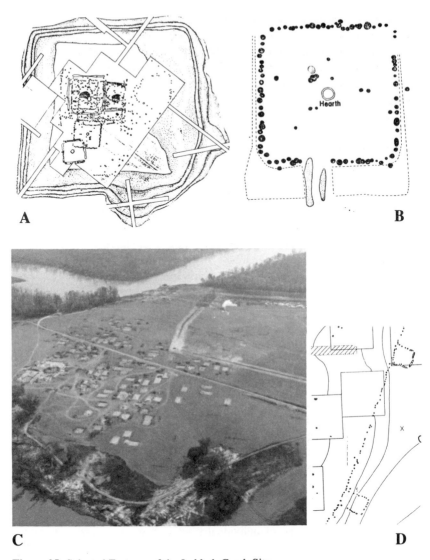

A

B

C

D

Figure 25. Selected Features of the Lubbub Creek Site

puddled clay hearth with a raised rim. The other was a two-roomed building with walls of closely spaced posts set into six wall trenches. The larger room was 7 m (23 ft.) square, the smaller measured 5 m (16.4 ft.) by 4 m (13.1 ft.) with an open short side. The smaller room also contained a basin-shaped centrally located hearth but it was poorly preserved (fig. 24, A). The last two structures in the mound precinct were superimposed upon and intruded into the remains of the earlier buildings. One of these, the earliest, was an 8 m (26.2 ft.) square structure with closely spaced wall posts set in individually dug holes. It had a basin-shaped centrally located hearth of puddled clay with a raised rim. Two parallel wall trenches extending from one side of this one-room building indicated the position of an entryway whose floor was built of prepared clay which had been hard packed through use (fig. 24, B). The latest structure, like one of its earlier counterparts, was a two-roomed building. It, however, had walls of closely spaced posts set in individual holes. The larger of the two rooms was 7.4 m (24.3 ft.) long and 6.7 m (23 ft.) wide. A rectangular baked clay platform 1.3 m long (4.3 ft.), 0.85 m wide (2.8 ft.), and 18 cm (7 in.) high lay in the center of this room. The smaller room, which measured 6.7 m (23 ft.) by 4.8 m (15.7 ft.), contained two baked clay platforms. The larger of these was circular. It was 2 m (6.6 ft.) in diameter and 20 cm (7.9 in.) high. The smaller was a low rectangle 1.4 m (4.6 ft.) long, 0.5 m (1.6 ft.) wide, and 8 cm (3 in.) high. The entire "mound precinct" was separated from the village area by a curtain wall of closely spaced individually set posts which at one time enclosed a 25 m (82 ft.) square and shielded all of the buildings within from public view (Peebles and Blitz 1981, 1–84).

The palisade at Lubbub Creek (fig. 24, D) and similar fortifications at other Moundville variant sites constitute reasonably good presumptive evidence for warfare or at least the expectation thereof. More direct evidence of conflict and military ventures comes from the excavation of a Summerville phase cemetery at Lubbub Creek (Jenkins and Ensor 1981). In addition to extended flesh interments, this particular cemetery contained the remains of a two-part circular enclosure with walls built of individually set closely spaced upright posts woven together by horizontal split-cane lathing and finished with a layer of clay plaster. This structure which was 13.5 m (44.3 ft.) in diameter encircled a group of four burials, two of which were of special interest by virtue of the southern cult paraphernalia with them. Both were primary extended interments of robust males in their early thirties, placed one atop the other and oriented east to west. The uppermost corpse had a triangular projectile point imbedded in his right chest at the time of burial. Both inhumations contained the dismembered remains, the arms, lower legs, and feet, of at least one, perhaps two, other individuals. These additional body parts were fleshed when laid in the grave, leading to their interpretation as war trophies (Hill 1981, 299, 278–80). The southern cult paraphernalia associated with these burials included a square copper plate embossed with a falcon and twelve copper projectile points (fig. 26, A–C). The latter were probably cut from embossed copper plates, since they carried fragmentary motifs (Ensor 1981). Three-quarters of a Moundville Incised var. *Moundville* pot was also found in the grave (Jenkins and Ensor 1981).

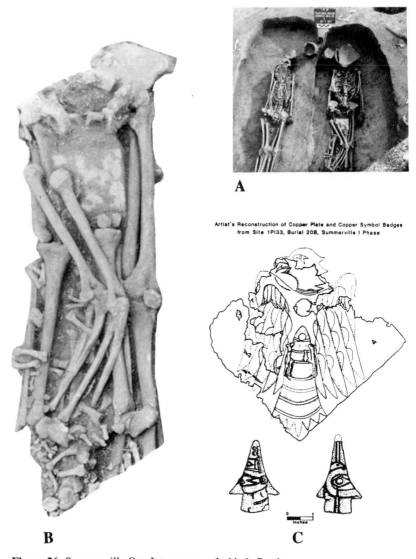

Artist's Reconstruction of Copper Plate and Copper Symbol Badges from Site 1Pi33, Burial 20B, Summerville I Phase

A

B   **C**

Figure 26. Summerville One Interments at Lubbub Creek

Chronology

The spatial spread of the Summerville One phase is not as clearly delimited as we might wish. To the east it overlaps with the Moundville One phase, and to the northwest with the Tibbee Creek phase (Marshall 1977). Its southern boundary, moreover, has yet to be set (fig. 24). Then again, it is presently impossible to assign many of the sites between Tibbee Creek and Lubbub Creek to phases. Summerville One has been assigned the interval between A.D. 1000 and A.D. 1200 by virtue of a substantial series of radiocarbon determinations (Peebles and Blitz 1981). Hence, it is fairly clear now that the Woodland and Mississippian occupation of the Tombigbee drainage overlapped by at least a century, giving us a rather comfortable cushion of time for conflict and acculturation between them.

The Summerville Two and Three Phases

Material Culture

For epistemological and evidentiary reasons Peebles and Mann (1981, 63) treated the Summerville Two and Three phases as an aggregate. We shall do likewise, adding the caveat that a future division should not only be possible but desirable. The ceramic technology established during Summerville One times continued, with minor modifications, until the 1500s. Mississippi Plain var. *Warrior* and Bell Plain var. *Hale* continued to be the dominant potteries. During Summerville Two and Three times, the number of strap handles customarily applied to Mississippi Plain var. *Warrior* doubled, increasing from two to four per vessel. This was apparently a continuing trend, for by the end of the Summerville Three phase the number of handles per vessel increased to six, eight, or sometimes even more. At about the same time, Alabama River Appliqué first appeared, albeit in minuscule quantities. This particular type did, however, become a distinctive feature of the later Summerville Four phase. There were also changes in the form of Bell Plain var. *Hale* during Summerville Two and Three. The ovoid pedestaled bottle was replaced by a bottle with a wider body and shorter pedestal or slab base (Moore 1905, figs. 35, 37, 39, 53). Pedestaled and slab bases disappeared later. The beaded or filleted rim was first made in Summerville Two times, Moundville Incised var. *Moundville* disappeared, and var. *Carrollton* became the dominant variety in Summerville Three. Carthage Incised var. *Moon Lake* continued to be made and vars. *Carthage* and *Fosters* appeared for the first time (Jenkins 1982, 135).

Subsistence Practices

In subsistence practices, settlement pattern, and lithic tool manufacture, Summerville Two and Three were reasonable facsimiles of their Summerville One ancestor. Maize was the dominant food plant, comprising more than 95 percent of all plant remains. Nuts constitute only 3 percent of the plant remains, hickory accounts for 95 percent of the nut shells, and acorns for most of the rest. Walnut and beechnut shells are rare. Passionflower, chenopodium, sedge, may grass, sage, reeds, and common beans (*Phaseolus vulgaris*) are also present (Caddell 1981b, 206, 213–14, 238). Mammals comprise 90 percent of the identified bone: deer bone is the most numerous. Birds and turtles contributed variety to the diet (Scott 1981, 229–42).

Settlement Pattern

The Summerville Two and Three settlement pattern can be described as a simple nuclear-centered type containing "a permanent center, with or without satellites. The center may be a self-supporting town, or a market, or a ceremonial place that serves as a focus for surrounding villages or hamlets. The center is not strikingly differentiated in content from its satellites except when its character is primarily ceremonial" (Beardsley et al. 1956, 141). In the vicinity of Lubbub Creek the populace lived in compact communities clustered around flat-topped temple mounds or mound complexes. The Summerville community itself was not fortified at this time (Peebles and Blitz 1981, 45), but others existing at the same time were, some of them elaborately so. There were as well farmsteads here and there as indicated by the Tibbee Creek site (O'Hear et al. 1981), the Kellogg site (Atkinson, Phillips, and Walling 1980), and 1Gr2 (Jenkins 1975a, 56–152; Jenkins and Ensor 1981, 19–36). Summerville Two and Three stonesmiths made the same range of tools and used the same techniques that their Summerville One ancestors did (Jenkins 1982, 135).

Summerville Two and Three phase house ruins have been excavated at Lubbub Creek (Peebles and Blitz 1981), Tibbee Creek (see fig. 27 for an example of variations in Mississippian square houses) (O'Hear et al. 1981), and the Kellogg site (Atkinson, Phillips, and Walling 1980). The remains of seven dwellings were explored at Lubbub Creek. Five of these were oval, two rectangular. The oval houses, which varied in long-axis dimensions from 5.5 m (19 ft.) to 7.5 m (24.6 ft.), had walls of closely spaced individually set, upright posts. In three of the five cases these uprights had been interlaced with split-cane lathing and plastered inside and out with prepared clay. In the other two, the wall posts were not interlaced or plastered over, leading to the speculation that they may have been incomplete, special-purpose structures, or perhaps summer dwellings. One oval house differed from the others in having an inner circle of large posts and an outer circle of smaller uprights. Another had a semisubterranean floor with a central hearth but a very poorly defined post pattern—eight posts in no obvious alignment. The two rectangular structures were built of individually set posts, enclosing floors 7.5 m (24.6 ft.)

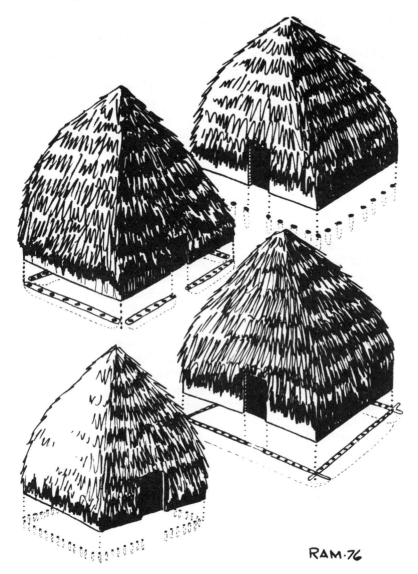

Figure 27. Artist's Recreation of Mississippian Square Houses Based upon Evidence from the Lyons Bluff Site

wide and 8 m (26.2 ft.) long. Both had entrances of wall trench type, but neither had clay plastered walls (Peebles and Blitz 1981). A rectangular two-roomed house of wall trench type was excavated by O'Hear et al. (1981) at the Tibbee Creek site, and two oval dwellings with walls of individually set posts which were not lathed and plastered were explored at the Kellogg site (Blakeman 1975, 96). One of these contained a central hearth, the other had three subfloor burials. Radiocarbon determinations on charcoal from these houses yielded dates of 1195±90 (Atkinson, Phillips, and Walling 1980, 233–37).

Chronology

The temporal and spatial dimensions of the Summerville One and Two phase composite are reasonably clear. To the east in the Black Warrior valley they overlap with the Moundville Two and Moundville Three phases. To the west and north they overlap with the Lyons Bluff phase (Marshall 1977, 56–57). The southern limit lies at or near 1Gr2, where a Summerville farmstead and cemetery have been excavated (Jenkins 1982, 138). The northern limits of a Summerville Two and Three occupation are unclear, but the middle Tennessee valley was occupied by peoples of the closely related Kogers Island phase centered on the Kogers Island, Perry, Little Bear Creek, McKelvey, and Seven Mile Island sites (fig. 24) (Webb and DeJarnette 1942 and 1948). The temporal position of the Summerville composite is well documented by a series of radiocarbon dates from the central Tombigbee valley; these range from A.D. 1185±90 to A.D. 1410±45 (Atkinson, Phillips, and Walling 1980, 196; Blakeman 1975, 96; Jenkins 1981, 34; and Peebles and Blitz 1981, 281). Hence, we estimate the duration to have been from A.D. 1200 to A.D. 1450. In fact, all of these Moundville variant phases are so similar that it is difficult to determine where the artifact assemblage of one ends and the other begins (see Jenkins 1982, 138–39).

5. Conclusion and Interpretations

Taxonomic Concerns

In the preceding chapters we purposely cultivated a narrow tract of prehistory—the Tombigbee drainage. Nevertheless, we treated the Tombigbee watershed not as an isolate but as a microcosm, a restricted universe but one within which the events and processes that shaped the broader sweep of southeastern prehistory could be better understood. We sought the patterning detectable in the materials of prehistoric archaeology, the trends and trajectories to be seen in our data. Ours was, therefore, a conscious attempt to delineate the continuities and discontinuities in our universe of discourse, to create through taxonomic means a synthesis of the data available. In pursuing this goal, we first discussed the taxonomic properties of aspects, foci, components, stages, periods, variants, phases, traditions, and horizons.

We wished to interpret our taxonomic units in the light of a general theory of evolution which could provide functional explanations for the growth, fixation, or loss of variety in cultural systems. We argued that the Midwestern Taxonomic System, popular in the third, fourth, and fifth decades of the twentieth century, created archaeological units which were best treated as material isolates. Since evolution does not act upon material isolates but upon spatially and temporally interrelated communities, we chose not to use the components, foci, and aspects of the Midwestern Taxonomic System. We also avoided the taxonomic use of currently popular schemes based in a succession of ethnologically derived ideal types like bands, tribes, chiefdoms, and so on. We have used the term *chiefdom* sparingly and as a descriptor, not a taxon. Our position on this point merely extends the caveats tendered by others vis-à-vis the use of ethnographic analogy. We share Wolf's (1982, 76) view that "most of the societies studied by anthropologists (from which such ideal types as bands, tribes, and chiefdoms were created) are an outgrowth of the expansion of Europe and not the pristine precipitates of past evolutionary states." We have, therefore, tried to avoid treating them as such. Instead we have chosen a taxonomic system which need not be encumbered by the vicissitudes of ethnographic analogizing and one that could be used to sketch continuities in time and space; namely, the Willey and Phillips Phase-Tradition-Horizon system. Further, we chose to add a midrange integrative taxon (the variant) to the system, and for articulating our subareal synthesis with those of broader scope, we retained the period and stage as classificatory devices.

We did, however, find it necessary to explicate our use of the concepts phase, tradition, horizon, variant, and stage. We interpreted phases as system states, multicommunity institution-channeled energy, matter, and information exchange climaxes. Traditions we construed as suprainstitutional information exchange routes and horizons as suprainstitutional matter and energy exchange nets. For us, variants were institution-channeled system trajectories, coherent flows of matter, energy, and information which occurred in time, in space, or in both. Finally, we argued that insofar as stages were considered parts of a sequent and inexorable series, they were inappropriate as taxa in the Southeast. We objected to the inevitability of state and empire formation that seemed implicit in this view, preferring instead the idea of a non-nuclear quasi series, the components of which were developmental only in the sense of being differing modes of adjustment to the Southeast's woodland environment. We have thus cast our lot with those who consider the discernible trends and trajectories in southeastern prehistory as evidence for a pattern of development which is "non-nuclear," that is, a set of social, political, and economic adjustments which, once established, impeded rather than promoted the spread of state and empirehood (Caldwell 1958, Dye 1980). We will argue presently that the Hopewell and Mississippian manifestations discussed herein represented culture climaxes, pinnacles of momentum gathered, examples of the ultimate in the expressed potential of social, economic, and political structures which could, in and of themselves, have gone no further than they did.

In the first substantive chapter of our work we created a regional taxonomic edifice composed of (1) the Gulf Formational stage; (2) three sequent Gulf Formational periods, Early (2500 to 1000 B.C.), Middle (1000 to 500 B.C.), and Late (500 to 100 B.C.); and in the western range of the region four variants (Bayou La Batre, Poverty Point, Wheeler, and Alexander), each of which expressed a different equilibrium state. We integrated all four of these variants in time via the Gulf Tradition and three of them in space via the widespread existence of a steatite trade, which we construed as a horizon. The subregional (i.e., Tombigbee watershed) taxonomic structure was embedded in its regional superstructure via the phases of the Wheeler and Alexander variants. We argued, for instance, that the Wheeler spatial variant ran through and united the Broken Pumpkin Creek phase with the Bluff Creek phase to the north. The Alexander spatial variant did the same for the Henson Springs phase.

In the second chapter we argued that in the Tombigbee drainage the Woodland stage followed the Gulf Formational and preceded the Mississippian. We divided the Woodland stage into Early (1000 to 100 B.C.), Middle (100 B.C. to A.D. 650), and Late (A.D. 650 to A.D. 1000) periods. We noted that in the Tombigbee drainage the Woodland stage opened in the Middle period with the advent of newcomers from the north. The Tombigbee was further seen as the home of two temporal variants during the Woodland stage, the Miller variant of the Middle period and the Baytown variant of the Late period. The phases of the Miller variant were integrated in time by the Northern and Middle Eastern ceramic traditions first proposed by Caldwell. These two ceramic traditions also ran through and united the Miller variant with its Baytown successor. The Hopewellian horizon tied Miller variant phases to their eastern and western contemporaries; a lapse into regionalism, then localism, accompanied the spatial spread of the Baytown variant. The Miller temporal variant integrated the Miller One phase (100 B.C. to A.D. 300) and its Bynum, Pharr, and Craigs Landing subphases with the Miller Two phase (A.D. 300 to A.D. 600) and its early Tupelo and later Turkey Paw subphases. The Baytown variant integrated the Miller Three phase (A.D. 600 to A.D. 1100) of the Tombigbee locality with its Deasonville and McKelvey counterparts elsewhere. The Miller Three phase was, in turn, divided into four subphases—Vienna, Catfish Bend, Cofferdam, and Gainesville.

The Mississippian stage was the last girder in our taxonomic superstructure. We divided it into Early (A.D. 1000 to A.D. 1250), Middle (A.D. 1250 to A.D. 1350), and Late (A.D. 1350 to 1450) periods and introduced the Moundville variant to join the Moundville One, Two, and Three phases with the Summerville One, Two, and Three phases and the Lyons Bluff One, Two, and Three phases. The tradition which ran through, united, and hence integrated the phases of the Moundville variant in time had as its core the manufacture of both coarse and fine shell-tempered ceramics and the Moundville ceramic series. These phases were joined in space by the spread of the symbol-rich ceremonialism of the southern cult.

These then are the temporal warps and spatial wefts in the fabric of prehistory in the Tombigbee watershed. We presume they will render us adequate assurance that the artifacts, artifactual residues, and the manufacture and use events we infer from them lie in their proper order. But we wanted our taxonomic structure to do a bit more. We wanted it to outline the flows of information, matter, and energy that gave shape to prehistoric social processes. We think it accomplished these ends reasonably well but we also realize that flows of matter, energy, and information are an integral part of fields of action and interaction. We suspect that such fields existed among spatially and temporally interrelated communities in the Tombigbee watershed, but to give them a modicum of interpretive import will require use of the concept of adaptation. Thus, in our view, a given adaptation is the consequence of interaction among a temporally and/or spatially related group of communities, the mode of production which characterizes each, and the adjustment each has made or is making to its environment. Before we proceed, however, we must clarify our understanding of two of these variables—namely, mode of production and adaptation—separately and in greater detail.

Conceptual Concerns

By mode of production we mean the way labor and technology are organized and deployed in a community (Wolf 1982, 73–77). A given mode of production thus gives shape and substance to the political and economic relationships that orient and constrain key social relations. Used synchronically the concept of mode of production focuses attention on variations in political and economic arrangements in space. It allows us to visualize their coterminous effects in similar and contrastive environments. Used temporally the concept forces us to evaluate the transformation from one variation to another within the same mode of production, or to seek reasons for the replacement of one mode of production by another. In our universe of discourse we may characterize the mode of production common to all communities from earliest to latest as based on kinship. Nevertheless, to do so in a clear and consistent manner will require (1) a statement detailing our particular construal of what kinship is and (2) a discussion of how kinship ties may be extended to form the ideological blueprint for distributing rights in and over persons and things.

We are among those who assume that kinship is based on human biological and social needs (see Schneider 1972). Kinship in our construal depends upon three biological facts: (1) human females bear relatively few young at a time; hence an extremely high rate of infant mortality cannot be easily tolerated; (2) human infants are helpless for a relatively long time; therefore they must be fed, sheltered, and protected for an extended period; and (3) humans reach sexual maturity relatively late in their lives and thus experience a prolonged period of biological and social dependency. In other words, children are born helpless and must be nurtured for a long period before they can assume a productive role in the community. Perhaps this is an overly complex way of saying that humans are not biologically wired to behave properly. They must be socially programmed to do so.

Social programming, however, takes social programmers. That is to say, some adults must be identified and committed to the tasks of child care and enculturation. A universal and distinctly human means for achieving this end (i.e., the identification of those adults responsible for child care) has been sought and found in the idea of presumed biological continuity (see Goodenough 1970, 3–38). Those adults presumed to share the essential relationship of biological continuity (however this may be conceptualized, symbolized, and understood) with nonadults are identified as their parents by descent (see Fortes 1953). In this view relatives by descent are those persons, adult and child, joined by parent-child links whether these be interpreted as taking matrilateral, patrilateral, or bilateral form. We reserve the expression *relatives by affiliation* for those adults linked to children (and made responsible for them) by virtue of an affinal tie to the parent by descent. Thus, we may distinguish between parents by descent and parents by affiliation. Finally, we construe full siblings as children with at least one common parent by descent. It should be obvious, therefore, that a parent by descent link is primary: affiliation and sibling links are secondary. This is so because the recognition of affiliation requires the existence of a prior marriage tie, and siblingship the prior existence of a descent link.

A differential command of resources and benefits inheres in parent-child links whether these be determined by descent or affiliation (see Radcliffe-Brown 1950, 1–85). The long period of infant care and enculturation previously noted requires that food, shelter, and protection be provided through descent- or affiliation-based claims on the time and labor of adults. Such claims seem always to be reciprocal whether translated into long- or short-term social indebtedness. Thus children (in a metaphorical sense) must borrow against their potential as independent agents and unencumbered producers. They must limit and/or place liens against their future productivity by creating an unfavorable ratio of labor owed to productive potential. In this metaphorical sense, then, we may claim that all human children incur a social debt as a consequence of their biological needs (Radcliffe-Brown 1950, 27).

It is through and by social indebtedness that superordination/subordination relations are created and maintained, and through the extension of these relations that authority is distributed within and sometimes among communities (see Leach 1961). Parent-child ties may be extended to form descent lines; sibling ties may be used to reach kinsmen in collateral lines of descent, and affiliative ties may be drawn upon for access to nonconsanguineal kin. Affinal linkages (i.e., marriage links) among descent-related groups of persons may also extend and strengthen preexisting superordination/subordination relations through the institution of bridewealth. Female children (again speaking metaphorically) must borrow against both their reproductive independence and labor potential to pay the social indebtedness incurred in childhood. This indebtedness is often realized through a male parent's claim to hold a monopoly over his daughter's reproductive potential. This monopoly can be and often is transferred to a woman's husband via the payment of bridewealth. But most prospective husbands must first borrow from relatives to pay the bridewealth without which they cannot themselves acquire a monopoly over their wife's reproductive power. In such cases, the need for bridewealth extends the prospective husband's prior indebtedness and strengthens the economic import of those parent-child (whether descent or affiliatively determined) and sibling ties he draws upon (Goodenough 1970, 13–17). If, with the help of relatives, a husband can manage the bridewealth payments and secure the unencumbered transfer of rights in and over his wife's offspring, his wife and her children will in turn owe him a share of their social indebtedness, and the pattern of subordination/superordination inhering therein will replicate itself. Even if bridewealth demands are modest, as they were among many historic native American groups, they still force the prospective husband to expend social or material wealth (i.e., weaken his economic or political position, if only temporarily) and encourage him to strengthen his ties to kinsmen as a hedge against future reverses. In sum, we see the web of kinship as an infrastructure which human ambition, individual initiative, and a host of other forces, both external and internal, may shape into a mode of production.

To return to our archaeological universe, there can be little doubt that ancient communities in the Tombigbee watershed were aggregates of consanguineal (descent-related), affiliative, and affinal kinsmen. That is, each community contained clusters of persons organized by virtue of interlocked parent-child and sibling ties, each related to others of similar kind by virtue of affinal links and affiliative parenthood. In short, each community contained a network of interlocking affinal, descent, affiliative, and sibling ties that served as the charter for the differential distribution of rights and duties, privileges, and obligations. Thus, through kinship, rights and duties were distributed to form an implicit labor-management system which was solidly embedded in particular relations among people. Nevertheless, the ways such rights and duties were spread within and among clusters of relatives varied a bit from place to place and time to time.

Later we shall argue that there were at least two contrastive prehistoric labor-management systems in the Tombigbee drainage, one based on consumable wealth which was widely available and open to anyone with the ability to obtain it and one based on durable wealth whose management was restricted to persons with a proper kinship claim. In the former instance authority grew from the give-and-take of daily life and depended upon performance for legitimacy and efficacy. In the latter instance, authority depended upon carefully drawn and enforced kinship-based restrictions on the right to manage labor or resources. In the first case each person, theoretically at least, held an equal share in the mode of production, and the group's technology was geared to treat the natural environment as an "object of labor" (Marx 1977, 284–85). In the second case, persons held unequal shares in the mode of production, and the group's technology converted some elements of the natural environment into instruments, or facilities, of labor. Let us now detail our understanding of adaptation.

That relationship between technology, social practice, and the environment which promoted the expansion or persistence of a population at the expense of its competitors shall be termed *adaptation*. But, unless technology and environment alone determine the rest of culture, there is latitude for variation in the social forms associated with a given pattern of adaptation. One problem confronting the archaeological study of prehistoric peoples is, then, the selection of those aspects of social life which are functionally related to environmental variables. Another, perhaps more important, problem lies in determining which of these relations have demonstrable adaptive significance.

Steward (1938), Netting (1965, 87), and others have suggested that the density and distribution of population together with the size, composition, distribution, and degree of permanency of settlements have verifiable adaptive significance in most environmental contexts. To these factors may be added the role of the sexes, the role of the family, and the composition and size of communal groups formed for such economic enterprises as hunting, gathering, fishing, or farming (Krause 1970, 103–14). It is to these social aggregates that entrepreneurial and management efforts must be directed and through them that such efforts realize gain. Together they form the complex of factors in Steward's (1955, 37) "culture core" and the "social instrumentalities" discussed by Netting (1965, 86). Nevertheless, the possibility of independent variation among factors is strong enough and the interfactor relationship complex enough to make separate treatment an analytical desideratum.

A few examples of the complexity of interfactor relationships may be instructive. A region's natural resources may set an upper limit to, but do not determine, population density. While it is true enough that in technologically simple hunting and gathering societies the food yield per acre is frequently small and the population density relatively low, even a cursory inspection of population maps will show that agriculture is not invariably accompanied by greater population densities. Factors other than technology and environment must be called upon to explain such situations. The tendency for agriculture to be preceded by and result in population increases may, for instance, be balanced by cultural practices affecting health and fertility, morbidity, or fecundity. Then, too, effective use of technological capabilities may be hampered by the accuracy and extent of traditional knowledge about or attitudes toward climatic, edaphic, and biotic factors (Krause 1970, 104–105).

Still other cultural and economic forces may shape significant social alignments. Endemic warfare may influence the areal distribution of a population as well as alter the age and sex composition of villages, households, and communal work groups. Involvement in trade may put a premium on the drawing together of interdependent craftsmen, may induce the participants to settle along trade routes, or may reshape the traditional economic role of the sexes (Krause 1967, Trigger 1963 and 1965). Finally, historical factors must not be neglected. Patterns of social life, which evolved in one area, may be transferred to another and only slowly modified to suit conditions in the new region (Krause 1970, 110–14). In sum, each and every factor bears close examination in each and every case.

The remainder of our concluding chapter will deal (by example) with the fit between our interpretations of the various taxa within the Lehmer-modified Willey and Phillips system and a general theory of evolution which leads us to seek functional explanations for the growth, fixation, or loss of variety in operationally defined systems. As a logical bridge between our taxonomic units and a general theory of evolution we shall use the previously discussed ideas of adaptation, field of interaction, and mode of production. We shall construe adaptation as an ex post facto judgment about the persistence or growth of a particular set of social practices vis-à-vis its competitors. We consider our use of the idea to be logically consistent with our interpretation of the taxon variant. We see the competition in question as occurring within a specific field of interaction created by the spread of populations, ideas, or goods. As such, it forms a logical fit with our construal of the taxon horizon. Insofar as the result of the competition is the modification or replacement of a preexisting mode of production (which we *identify* by virtue of our interpreta-tion of the taxon tradition) we shall consider it a significant processual event, a springboard for invigorating older forms of social dynamism or creating new potentials upon which other forces may act to shape those transformations of social, political, and economic life which we have identified as stage markers (given our interpretation of stages as parts of a quasi series). We shall not explicitly restate these relationships in the remainder of our discussion, prefer-ring instead to leave them implicit in what we say and do. With these caveats in mind let us turn our attention to that region east of the Mississippi River classed as the eastern woodlands.

Processual Concerns

If Quimby (1954) is right, some of the earliest inhabitants of the eastern woodlands followed a pancontinental coniferous zone into the northeastern forests and worked their way southward. Quimby's forest-adapted immigrants may well have settled the Northeast, but it seems reasonable to suppose that lands to the south may have been settled from the plains. T. Lewis (1954) noted a correlation between fluted-point occurrences in the Southeast and the distribution of relic prairies. He inferred an eastward spread of grasslands during the altithermal as well as an eastward spread of big-game hunters. Some of the first comers to the Southeast may, indeed, have brought with them a hunting and harvesting tradition shaped by prior experience with a plains or prairie environment. Hence we may expect an initial pattern of single elephant kills at favored hunting stations in relic prairie lands. Nevertheless, with the disappearance of the elephant in the East we should not expect a shift to the plains grassland pattern of herd animal hunting (i.e., mass kills resembling drives or pounds, and opportunistic surrounds in the breaks along water courses or drainage ways). We may expect instead a fine-tuning of the hunting and harvesting economy geared to increasing efficiency in using the forest. This fine-tuning should be manifested in the emergence of (1) a forest analogue to grassland forms of ambush hunting, (2) seasonal cycles of movement and resource use expressing a forest rhythm, and (3) the discovery and use of new forest-based sources of natural plant and animal foods. Our Tombigbee sample indicates this does, in fact, seem to be the pattern discernible in the eastern Archaic stage. This pattern's social implications need further attention.

The forest-adapted version of grassland ambush hunting would of necessity be focused upon solitary game animals like deer. In this respect it would resemble the earliest elephant-hunting pattern. Elephant hunting would, however, require more hunters per animal than would deer hunting. Thus, we might expect that the forms of task allocation and reward disbursement that characterized an elephant hunt during the chase and after were different from those typifying the smaller hunting party or single-hunter deer kills. For elephant hunts all participants probably received immediate rewards, each according to his contribution as that was socially defined. Thus, experienced hands may have received a larger share than their less-capable counterparts, but each participant, in most cases all healthy adult male household or residence group heads, received a portion of the kill. Under these circumstances, such social indebtedness as existed would be ephemeral. It would have been difficult, indeed, to build a political or managerial power base by creating an elephant meat debt and/or credit chain. When elephant meat was available, it was available to all. Deer hunting, however, was a different matter. Single hunters or small hunting parties (by no means including all able-bodied hunters in a group) were sufficient to seek and obtain deer. We might further suspect that the incidence of success for such endeavors would be sufficiently irregular as to produce temporary meat surpluses for a few but not all members of a community. Such meat surpluses could, and we presume would, provide the raw materials for building at least ephemeral forms of social debt and credit.

Gulf Formational Events and Processes

As early as Broken Pumpkin Creek phase times, perhaps earlier, prehistoric populations in the Tombigbee were composed of woodland-adapted hunting and gathering groups using portable tools, weapons, implements, and containers. We previously argued for a division of labor by age and sex with decision making by consensus. The role of the leader most probably fell to the adult male most capable of shaping and expressing a consensus. A kind of balanced reciprocity is the typically dominant form of economic integration in such groups, and in native North America this kind of economic integration was achieved through the custom of honoring by gift giving (see Holder 1970). With communities the size of those posited for Broken Pumpkin Creek peoples, the exchange of gifts could have moved goods and services through co-resident domestic groups with relative ease and efficiency, and, insofar as the goods moved via gift exchange were consumable (like deer meat), and insofar as a return in service or kind was demanded by local custom, gift giving could form the basis for political action.

Presents of meat and other consumables, if not immediately returned, put the receiver in the donor's debt. Hence, these exchanges could be manipulated by experienced and ambitious hunters to place consanguineal and affinal kinsmen in their debt and render them more amenable to consensus-building efforts. When decision making by consensus was focused upon a daily and annual round of economic practices (i.e., when one man's interpretation of plant and animal behavior was valued above his competitors), political success could be measured by the number of domestic groups a man could attract and hold from season to season and year to year as he moved himself and his followers to food.

Leadership by consensus is, however, ephemeral and by its very nature can serve only a population of limited size and permanence. To build and maintain a consensus-based following greater than ten domestic groups would require extraordinary skill and effort. Thus, in consensus-based groups, authority tends to be impermanent. The strong leader of a season might, through a series of reverses, become a mere follower within the passage of a yearly round. What is more, membership in such groups tends to be no more permanent than leadership. Separate domestic groups aggregate for common cause during greater or shorter periods of time, depending upon the issues at hand and the success or lack thereof of those in power. Such groups fragment with population growth, congeal when suitable reserves of wild food are available, dissipate when they are not, and usually melt away in the face of better-organized and more vigorous competitors.

Thus, in consensus-governed groups food and goods (locally produced or traded in) do not go to maintain a stratified social order or codified authority structure. In such groups the shibboleth of giving has individual consequences. After a lucky hunt, or success in a trading venture, an ambitious man might find himself rich with an abundance of meat or trade goods, but this wealth would shortly be given to others and there were no stable ranked groups to channel its flow. The fortunate entrepreneur might raise his status to the highest in the group by making himself poor through prestations. Shortly, however, there would be a return in service or in kind from others who were intent upon raising their own status. Thus, the overall distribution of wealth benefited the whole group, provided the basis for political action, but committed no one to a stable political order and actually inhibited the creation of a codified authority structure. In sum, continued success in providing and distributing meat and other consumables was the most stable underpinning of a political order which would have proved weak, at best, in the face of a prolonged external threat or challenge.

The pattern of leadership typical of Broken Pumpkin Creek peoples probably continued during the Henson Springs phase, bringing with it status mobility, shifting group and political allegiances, and the manipulation of consumable wealth as a means to political ends. There had, however, been a modest growth in the degree of dependence upon externally generated sources of durable wealth, some of which was being consumed in the burial practices attributed to the Broken Pumpkin Creek phase participants in the Pickwick burial complex. External wealth had been available to Broken Pumpkin Creek populations as indicated by the extent and duration of the steatite trade, but they seemed more the receivers than the manipulators of the flow. During Broken Pumpkin Creek times goods and raw materials seem to have flowed from the fall line to the coast via coastal plain rivers, providing Poverty Point peoples a source of durable wealth to manipulate. By Henson Springs phase times a far more modest, yet nonetheless real, flow of wealth was apparently channeled north and south via the Tombigbee drainage, perhaps giving Henson Springs phase peoples more wealth to manipulate than their predecessors. Nevertheless, it was still apparently of insufficient import to modify the prevailing pattern of status mobility or to solidify a nascent authority structure. These limitations we suspect proved to be shortcomings in the face of competition from newcomers who brought with them a different political and work management system—a new social order whose organizing ideology lay in a complex mortuary ritual and whose economic strength lay in trade ties with a parent population to the north. We have identified these newcomers as the authors of the Miller variant, more specifically, the bearers of the Miller One phase.

Woodland Events and Processes

Earlier we suggested that the peoples who produced Miller One phase remains entered the Tombigbee drainage from the north. In other words, we were positing an immigration. We realize, however, that arguing the immigration thesis will require (1) identifying a suitable parent population, (2) presenting a case for close parallels in material culture between presumed parent and offspring, (3) showing that the immigration in question was but one of several contemporaneous movements of people in the same region and in the same direction (i.e., indicating that the case at hand was part of a more general process), (4) detailing a suitable migration route, and (5) giving a reasonable account of what happened to the region's indigenes.

Miller-like manifestations are to be found north of the Tombigbee, where they constitute the Pinson complex. The central and largest Pinson complex component, the Pinson mounds site, lies in the Tennessee uplands approximately 50 miles north of the Tombigbee headwaters, and only 10 to 15 miles west of the Tennessee-Mississippi drainage divide. The Pinson mounds site, itself, consists of 30 mounds (some of them surrounded by linear earthworks) and the associated detritus of day-to-day village life (Myer 1922, fig. 2). The mounds vary in size, but one of them, Sauls Mound, is the second tallest in North America. Most of the earthworks (Fisher and McNutt 1962, Mainfort 1980, Morse and Polhemus n.d. [a]) and Sauls Mound were constructed between 100 B.C. and A.D. 650 (personal communication from R. Mainfort, June 1981), but earlier and later materials may also be present. A radiocarbon assay of 200 B.C. provides evidence for earlier material; the suggestion of even later material is speculative. Nevertheless, by all measures now available the Pinson population existed at the proper time, was sufficiently large and vigorous, and was thoroughly capable of spawning offshoots like the people who produced the Miller remains a scant 50 miles to the south. Pinson, in fact, seems to be the largest Hopewellian center south of Ohio and Illinois and may have been a source for the spread of both peoples and mortuary ceremonialism.

Pinson material culture in general, and ceramic manufacture in particular, was very similar to that of their posited offspring—Miller One peoples among them. Pinson ceramics have been classified using types of both the Twin Lakes complex—that is, the Mississippi valley Marksville (Morse and Polhemus n.d. [a])—and the Miller One and Miller Two complexes (Fisher and McNutt 1962). Broster (1975) and Broster and Schneider (1975) also used both Miller and Twin Lakes types. Jenkins's (1982) examinations of Pinson ceramics, however, indicated they were virtually identical with Miller One and Miller Two wares, with the greatest difference being the infrequent tendency (10 percent or less) to include grog as a temper early in the Pinson sequence. Most of the early grog-tempered pottery was also very sandy with sparse ground sherd inclusions. Futhermore, recent excavations at the Pinson mound site indicate a sequence of change similar to that in the Miller One–Miller Two phase sequence:

> In the lowest level (Stratum VI), Saltillo Fabric Impressed is by far the dominant type present (73%). Furrs Cordmarked (9%), and Withers Fabric Marked (8%) are minority types, as is, surprisingly, Tishomingo Cordmarked (2%). It will be recalled that this was an undisturbed sealed component beneath the mound.
>
> Although a mixed deposit, Stratum V also represents premound occupation. The lowest level (level 2) yielded a ceramic collection with a lower frequency of Saltillo Fabric Impressed (50%) than Stratum VI, while Furrs Cordmarked (15%), Baldwin Plain (9%), Tishomingo Cordmarked (6%), Tishomingo Plain (1%), and Withers Fabric Marked (12%) increase. In level I of Stratum V, the percentage of Furrs Cordmarked (36%) increased markedly, while Saltillo Fabric Impressed (20%) is much less common. Other types showing increases are Baldwin Plain (16%), Tishomingo Cordmarked (13%), and Tishomingo Plain (5%), while Withers Fabric Impressed (2%) decreased. [Mainfort 1980, 43]

There are also similarities between Pinson and Miller (specifically Pharr site) burial programs. At Pinson, Mound 12 contained a series of platforms with crematories (Mainfort 1980, 22–24). These bear practical identity to the platform and crematory within Mound E at the Pharr site. Thus both burial programs emphasized the special ceremonial handling of the dead, more specifically the cremation of the corpse upon an earthen platform or altar, the incorporation of the cremated remains in the crematory altar, the inclusion of durable wealth as a mortuary offering when the crematory platform was sealed with a stratum of dirt or clay, and the covering of the sealed mortuary altar with a thicker layer of dirt also containing offerings and/or later extended or flexed flesh burials. To be sure, the superimposed crematoria in Mound 12 at the Pinson site indicate a more substantial population with greater persistence than at the Pharr site. Nevertheless, at any single time the burial programs were, for all intents and purposes, duplicates.

To this point we have argued that Miller One peoples produced pottery of the basic Pinson type, experienced a similar pattern of ceramic change (i.e., a transformation from the predominance of fabric-marked to cord-marked pottery), and conducted virtually identical mortuary programs. Thus, the close proximity of Miller and Pinson remains leads us to conclude that Pinson and Miller were related. That this relationship was one of Pinson as parent and

Miller as offspring is indicated by the general southward spread of the Pinson complex. We are positing that Miller peoples were but one of several offspring that may have been derived from a Pinson parent. We suspect that the Womack complex (Koehler 1966), the Boyd phase (Connaway and McGahey 1971), and the Twin Lakes phase (Phillips 1970, 891) of the lower Mississippi valley drainage were also Pinson derivates. Together with the Miller One phase they were collectively classed as the Miller variant, a vigorous population in dynamic equilibrium with their environment and in the process of spreading themselves and their ideas over a substantial portion of Mississippi and Alabama.

The avenue of movement for the peoples and ideas that formed the Miller variant was the hilly region that extended from west-central Tennessee southward to south-central Mississippi. The Pinson mounds site was within the west Tennessee Plain physiographic district, which extended southward into Mississippi where it joined the Mississippi North Central Hills district. The western portions of the North Central Hills were drained by the Coldwater, Tallahatchie, Yalobusha, Yocona, and Big Black Rivers, all of which debouched into the Mississippi. These rivers flowing out of the North Central Hills may have been routes for the movement of peoples and ideas that, among other things, led to the replacement of fabric-marked by cord-marked pottery. Ford (1952, 363–64) for instance, in his discussion of Withers Fabric Marked pottery, states:

> Withers is closely related to a group of similar types that form an important element of the early ceramics in the central part of the East. It seems quite certain that the type was diffused into this portion of the Mississippi Alluvial Valley region from the northeast rather than directly down the valley. The principal surge seems to have come from northeastern Mississippi, where Jennings had recorded a frequency of 66 percent for the directly comparable Saltillo Fabric Marked from site MLe 53. The valleys of the Tallahatchie and Coldwater Rivers may very well have been the principal route by which this influence entered the flood plain for they lead from this Mississippi hill country directly into the Sunflower and Memphis areas where it was most pronounced. The Withers in the flood plain near the mouth of these rivers is heavily sand tempered, like Saltillo Fabric Marked, but in other parts of the alluvial valley clay tempering (read grog) is found. It is interesting to note that the later paddle stamped wares (cordmarked) found in this part of the Mississippi Valley appear to have come from the same direction and to have followed the same route.

Phillips, Ford, and Griffin (1951, 73–75) and Phillips (1970) agree that cord- and fabric-marked pottery reached the Mississippi valley floodplain from the Northeast. The eastern edge of the North Central Hills was drained by the Tombigbee. Peoples making cord- and fabric-marked pottery and practicing a Hopewellian-derived mortuary ritual seem to have moved from the North

Central Hills into the Tombigbee drainage, where they produced the remains classified as the Miller One phase. Finally, since research in the Tombigbee and the Mississippi alluvial valley has failed to define a transition from the Alexander to the Miller variant, we presume that Alexander peoples were displaced, perhaps forced, southward to become part of a Bayou La Batre successor population in the south coastal plain, and/or they were pushed eastward into the Bankhead Forest area of northwestern Alabama. The only other acceptable alternative, at the moment, is an exceedingly rapid assimilation into the immigrant Miller population.

The Miller One immigrants brought with them a hunting and foraging pattern reminiscent of their Henson Springs brethren. Small, seasonally occupied villages, clusters of large round or oval, timber-framed, grass-, bark-, or hide-covered houses, were now to be found on suitable stretches of bottomland, but smaller, more dispersed encampments still bespeak a continuing need to move people to huntable and harvestable natural foods. New and improved means of collecting, harvesting, and fishing are indicated such that, on the whole, Miller One peoples seem less precariously established than those of the Henson Springs phase. This appearance may, of course, be more apparent than real. The appearance of stability is, nevertheless, conveyed by the stylistic precocity of ceramic productions, the consumption of wealth in burial ritual, and the creation of community monuments in the form of burial tumulii.

Miller One mortuary monuments in and of themselves seem to indicate a commitment to forms of social, economic, and political life having a firmer structure than that of their forerunners. It seems that in Miller One communities there were men who could channel the flow of wealth made available through trade, men who could traffic in a surplus of durables as well as consumables. We suppose that such trafficking was still accomplished through the practice of honoring by gift exchange, but now perhaps with a new twist that converted durables to consumables and focused the consequences of gift giving upon the abstract idea of collective spiritual welfare. What we are suggesting here is (1) that durable wealth could be accumulated through success in trade, warfare, or the manipulation of consanguineal and affinal ties and (2) that such wealth was consumed in a mortuary ritual which provided status and prestige for the investor and led to a command over community resources, if only temporarily so. Thus we are positing a dual role for Miller One burial mounds. On the one hand, we see them as public monuments of mounded earth containing the remains of the group's ancestors and evidence of its success in manipulating external sources of durable wealth. In this light they were community shrines, examples of a community's fund of prestige to which members could point with pride and in which members shared, if perhaps differentially. On the other hand, we may view these burial tumulii as organized and, we suspect, managed investments of community resources that were both stage settings for past public ritual and tokens of traditional forms of authority, as evanescent and potentially equalitarian as these may have been.

In theory, we suppose all men had equal access to the means of production and distribution necessary for wealth accumulation and its investment in mortuary ritual. In fact, we suspect that some were more successful than others and that such success was heritable in the sense that successful fathers tended to be a greater advantage to their offspring than unsuccessful ones. Thus, command over community resources and benefits may have tended to become frozen along family lines, providing social substance to the greater structuring of wealth flow most archaeologists presume inhered in Middle Woodland (i.e., Hopewellian) social systems. Be that as it may, what is important to our argument is that Miller One burial tumulii were the first public monuments in the Tombigbee—the first durable, tangible examples of status seeking and prestige distribution through a commitment to public works. Miller burial mounds grew by virtue of consuming both the bodies of the dead and the wealth of the living. They gave in return a means for creating, maintaining, and distributing those forms of status and prestige that made possible the management of natural and social resources. That these forms of management conferred competitive success upon Miller One newcomers and were in the short run sustained by extralocal trade ties is suggested by subsequent events.

By Miller Two times the Woodland populations in the Southeast were expanding, and if Miller One successes had not been based on ties to external sources of wealth we might expect yet more intense mortuary ritual and elaborate public works. Miller Two peoples, however, conducted an impoverished mortuary ritual. They were no longer using Hopewell-derived mortuary programs. Nor did they substitute locally contrived or locally elaborated crematory rites. More important, they no longer consumed externally produced forms of wealth. Emergent organizational problems were still, in part at least, handled through a commitment to the construction of earthen funerary monuments, but the source of externally derived wealth, the Hopewell interaction net, had collapsed. With the interruption of long-distance trade, as modest as it must have been, the Woodland communities of the Southeast (with the exception of Weeden Island) turned inward upon themselves. The entrepreneurial efforts engendered by long-distance trade could now be focused only on locally produced and regionally distributed goods. But there had been few if any locally developed craft specialists which might have supplied the durable wealth needed for the more elaborate forms of mortuary consumption. Without a supply of durable and manipulable external wealth to manage, the prestige distribution base founded on mortuary monuments could not be widened. There were now new limits to the economic growth and entrepreneurial efforts that local means of production and consumption could support. The net result was a simplified burial ritual with a concomitant reduction in the number of prestigious managerial possibilities. As population continued to grow, even fewer positions of power and prestige were to be available to ever-greater numbers of candidates, eroding, we suppose, the differential command over community resources and benefits that had emerged in the halcyon years of elaborate burial ritual. We also suspect that environmental factors were beginning to exert a leveling effect.

Despite the intense mortuary ceremonialism and nascent structuring of resource and benefit differentials, Miller One peoples alternated periods of sedentary life with intervals of wandering. Hence the centripetal pull of monument building had always been balanced by the centrifugal force of episodic wandering. Why, we might ask, had a fully sedentary lifestyle not been achieved? There should have been enough in the way of collectible forest products and huntable deer for all in most localities, not to mention the more modest, or second-line, resources—rodents, fish, shellfish, and crayfish among them. Forest foods, nuts in particular, could be stored against periods of want, and meat could be dried. But a continuing need for fresh meat and skins for blankets, robes, and clothing could not be thus satisfied. Nor could the local reserves of collectible non-nut foods be efficiently utilized by a sedentary populace. The local game animals and collectible non-nut foods would soon be exhausted by a fully settled population, and trips farther and farther afield could then be anticipated. The effort required in hunting and gathering would increase with the distance one had to go from a settlement, and transport would become something of a problem. It is in this light that a patterned alternation between periods of settled life and periods of mobile life would seem significant. This pattern would minimize the problems of transport when they would otherwise be most pressing and maximize the efficiency of hunting and collecting, but not without weakening attempts to translate the managerial effects of mortuary ritual into durably structured gains in social standing. With no dependable source of external wealth to buttress them, and the aforementioned environmental forces undermining them, it is no wonder that Miller One differentials in command over resources and benefits faded in Miller Two and disappeared by Miller Three times. The ephemeralization of managerial structures seems to be the price paid for primary forest efficiency. Yet once achieved, primary forest efficiency fostered an institutional structure and plan of organization which was superseded only by the advent of food production.

Mississippian Events and Processes

The emergence of intensive forms of food production in the southeastern United States is a matter of great interest and some debate. The debate centers less upon when than upon how crop growing reached the region. To recapitulate an earlier observation, there are three contrastive views: (1) about A.D. 1000, immigrant Mississippian farming populations displaced resident Woodland groups (Caldwell 1958, 54); (2) from A.D. 700 to 900, resident Woodland hunting and gathering groups were transformed (i.e., Mississippianized) through the diffusion of ideas and practices typical of crop-growing peoples in other regions (Griffin 1985); and (3) from A.D. 800 to 1000, a limited influx of cultivators introduced ideas and practices which transformed resident hunters and harvesters and stimulated a fusion of resident with immigrant to produce local versions of a Mississippian lifestyle (Jenkins 1976).

Arguing the first, or immigration, position will require (1) identifying a parent population from which the immigrant group(s) were derived, (2) adducing reasons for large-scale migration, (3) demonstrating that the Mississippian population of a locale was itself a site unit intrusion or was derived from one, and (4) showing that local Woodland populations were expelled. Advancing the second position (that the local Mississippian lifestyle constituted a diffusion-induced transformation) will require (1) identifying compatible Woodland predecessors, (2) demonstrating trajectories in Woodland manufacturing and economic practices which under suitable conditions could produce elements of succeeding lifestyles, and (3) isolating what Rouse (1958, 63–68) called "trait unit intrusions" which could stimulate Mississippianization. Defending the third proposal (limited immigration and immigrant-resident fusion) would require demonstrating that (1) there were suitable newcomers in the locality or region, (2) that immigrant and resident populations coexisted for a suitable span of time, (3) that an exchange of ideas between resident and immigrant was possible, and (4) that a fusion of Woodland resident with Mississippian migrant could explain those local transformations in subsistence, settlement, and manufacturing practices which elsewhere in the Southeast are identified as Mississippian.

We are convinced that the fusion of Woodland resident with Mississippian migrant best explains the spread of food production to and through the Tombigbee watershed. Our evidence for this conclusion includes (1) the coexistence of the late subphases of the Miller Three phase with the earliest phases of Mississippian life in the area; (2) a growth in the importance of maize cultivation late in the Miller Three phase; (3) the later Miller Three preference for rectangular thatched-roof houses with pole and mud-plaster walls over the dome-shaped pole, grass, and bark hut popular earlier; (4) the continued use of the Miller Three variety of Madison type projectile points during Mississippian times; (5) late Miller Three burial practices (extended or flexed flesh burials) which closely resemble their Mississippian counterparts; (6) the occurrence of shell and grog, and shell tempering of a Mississippian kind late in the Miller Three phase; and (7) the introduction of loop handles reminiscent of Mississippian forms in late Miller Three times. The faunal and floral use trends discernible in the Miller Three phase also square well with the minimal immigration maximal incorporation argument. We shall presently illustrate why, but first we must discuss our objections to the mass migration and stimulus diffusion arguments.

If food production was brought to the Southeast via large-scale immigration we might suggest that population pressure elsewhere was the motivating force, that farmable lands to the north and west were exhausted or in short supply. Thus if immigrant populations were reasonably large, they were, in effect, colonists fleeing the effects of population pressure in their homeland and ultimately subject to reincorporation by the parent population, if and when such became feasible. It never did, and we lack good evidence for overpopulated regions north and west of the Tombigbee. Further, if these putative colonial populations grew at a typical rate, and if Smith's (1978, 486) assertion that Mississippian peoples confined themselves to "linear, environmentally circumscribed floodplain habitats" is also correct, they should have filled the space available to them quite rapidly. Once the available space was filled, we might expect either programs of land improvement like those in Mexico or the southwestern United States, or competition for unimproved lands and unmanaged natural resources. We have little, if any, evidence for programs of land improvement or intensive natural resource management (see R. Lewis 1974). There were, however, elaborate fortifications around the larger Mississippian towns (Lafferty 1973).

Most archaeologists identify the fortification systems around Mississippian towns as a response to competition over unimproved lands and unmanaged resources. That such competition led to a raiding and feuding pattern of warfare seems a reasonable inference. But some see the bastioned fortification walls, guarded gateways, and dry moats of the Southeast as evidence for the emergence of conquest warfare (Larson 1972). If these scholars are right, then Mississippian peoples may have been taking the first faltering steps toward building conquest states. Reference to the developmental patterning discernible in other regions of North America does not, however, support this view. Fortifications of similar plan and construction appear in the northern plains at about the same time but plains specialists do not consider them evidence for wars of conquest (Lehmer 1971). Then, too, rather drastic defensive measures were taken by the prehistoric residents of the American Southwest. Here again, few would consider them evidence for attempts at conquest (Kidder 1968). In sum, the large-scale incorporation of vanquished by victor which presumably played a role in Mexican state building seems alien to the pattern of development north of the Rio Grande.

Griffin (1985, 61) discusses the migration hypothesis but clearly prefers the view that resident hunting and gathering groups were Mississippianized by the introduction of maize and the consequences of maize farming.

> While maize, which probably came from the Southwest, was known in the East by about A.D. 1, it was not a significant part of the food supply until the period A.D. 700–900, when it appeared in quantity over a wide area. Apparently it took more than a half-millennium to acquire adequate cultivation, seed-selection, food-preparation, and storage techniques to transform this crop into the valuable food supply it became in most of the prehistoric Eastern societies after A.D. 900. . . . Our view is that this major addition to their already sophisticated hunting and gathering skills permitted population growth, resulting in a need for mechanisms of societal control and thereby hastened the changes in societal structure.

The major questions raised by Griffin's interpretation are (1) why was the potential of full-scale maize cultivation unrealized for 500 years and (2) why was there a rapid growth in maize cultivation from A.D. 700 to 900. Truly definitive answers elude us for now, but as usual in such cases, potentially fruitful speculations may be advanced.

Most southeastern prehistorians have noted the abundance of the eastern forests and the progressively intense integration of natural plant and animal foods into the region's Archaic and Woodland economies (see Caldwell 1958). For millennia the Southeast seems to have been like the Pacific Coast. Its human population was in dynamic equilibrium with its food supply. To be sure, technological innovations may, from time to time, have increased the natural foods available, and human populations, as a consequence, may have grown until a new balance was struck. Nevertheless, people still moved to food with the rhythm and range of such movement determined, in part, by human knowledge of the distribution and behavior of plants and animals. Under such circumstances, the introduction of maize via trade or diffusion would render it an oddity. That maize could be grown or tended may have been realized from the outset. But full-scale cultivation would have hindered the efficiency of established and successful subsistence practices. Maize in limited quantitites may have been tangentially incorporated into Woodland economies, perhaps as an item of religious attention or as a delicacy, in those regions where the abundance and close geographical juxtaposition of natural foods stimulated the greatest degree of residential stability. Full-scale cultivation would, however, require a narrowing of the range of intense natural resource use and greater residential stability than most groups had achieved prior to about A.D. 700 or 800. It is from this perspective that the faunal and floral trends in the Miller Three phase seem to square with the minimal immigration–maximal incorporation explanation.

If a limited influx of cultivators did introduce new ideas and practices to the Tombigbee, we might expect them to force a narrower range of intensive resource use upon the Woodland residents, especially in those areas of greatest population density. By Miller Three times, the Tombigbee drainage seems to have been sustaining peak hunting and harvesting populations. If immigrants had moved into this area, they would have claimed economically important riverbottom territories for their own use. A part of the area would thus be removed from the reach of resident hunters and harvesters creating an intense, if local, disruption of the natural resource/population balance. Hunting and gathering groups could temporarily redress the problem by using second-line resources, as some apparently did, or they could seek a longer-term solution by extending the range of their hunting and harvesting grounds. This latter solution would in its turn disrupt the balance between population and natural resources in a broader area, thus putting pressure on neighboring groups to either extend their territory or narrow their range of intense natural resource use. Such pressure should encourage intergroup competition and conflict. If some of the populous and settled groups, in an attempt to retain the advantage of massed manpower, responded by intensifying the harvesting portion of their subsistence cycle, then crop growing might provide them a minimally disruptive alternative to intense, if periodic, overuse of harvestable wild foods. An increased commitment to crop growing could then provide the impetus for partial Mississippianization, which itself might prepare the way for full-scale incorporation into a Mississippian lifestyle via the vehicle of continued population growth and additional narrowing of the resource range. In short, competition, conflict, and a preadaptive response wave may have preceded the advent of cultivators in a given region, easing their acquisition of new lands and adding substantially to their natural rate of population increase. Further, if the newly expanding cultivating populace continued to grow and spread, the process would feed upon itself, gaining momentum as it occurred in one region after another until the "linear environmentally circumscribed floodplain habitats" of the Southeast were filled. There would still be territories beyond the effective reach of cultivators which might have remained hunter and harvester strongholds. Indeed, the continued presence of a potentially hostile hunting and harvesting folk may have been an ancillary impetus for the construction of Mississippian fortifications.

Thus, in respect to the advent of food production in the Tombigbee drainage, we are not so much positing mass migration (which implies the long-distance movement of people in some numbers) as we are modest population growth and the minimal, short-distance spread of people which might accompany it. In our model the major mover is the transformation of a hunting-harvesting economy by virtue of forced narrowing of the resource range. To be sure, we posit the intrusion of a few newcomers, but we do so from a purely local perspective; that is, the newcomers are from nearby (the next valley perhaps), and they are southeasterners who themselves have not been food producers for long. We are, in effect, positing a kind of multiplex chain reaction which began at some distance from the Tombigbee drainage and well before we see evidence of it in our materials. The reaction reached our domain of discourse through multiple and various routes and via numerous prior interactions and transformations. We see events in the Tombigbee as but local links in a tortuous and sinuous multilinked chain of events whose ultimate source lay to the north and west.

Settled populations tied to a reasonably narrow range of intensively used resources pose managerial problems. Among them are the need to adjudicate disputes, allocate land, organize and direct labor, and regulate the flow of food and other commodities. Peebles (1974) and others (Steponaitis 1978; Walthall 1980, 246–76) argue that Mississippian social systems were chiefdoms—regionally centralized organizations of ranked communities in which social position was determined by genealogical distance from a real or mythical ancestor. In the oldest, largest, and politically most mature settlements, genealogical distance from the paramount chief determined the local distribution of status and prestige. This principle was extended to include and incorporate smaller, less mature satellite villages and hamlets such that the rank of each depended in turn upon a person's genealogical distance from his or her local authority. Thus, order was based on a hierarchical series of social and territorial groups—the village, the district, and chiefdom, with the highest-ranking member of each local community being the local chief or headman; the highest-ranking local chief being the district chief; and the highest-ranking district chief being the paramount. Chiefs at all levels had broad rights of request for food, goods, and services, while being generally responsible for their followers' welfare. Each chief, subchief, or village headman served as the conduit for decisions made at higher levels, decisions which involved him in the recruitment of labor for socially beneficial projects, the conduct of war or trade, the organization of religious festivals, and/or the mediation of disputes among group members. For most, tribute and support of elite activities were kinship obligations. In return for their contributions of wealth or service, commoners participated in the prestige gained by their elite kinsman's manipulation of wealth, organization of raids, or conduct of religious ceremonies. Thus, rulers and ruled alike were caught up in a social fabric of mutual obligation reenforced by the threads of economic interdependence and kin allegiance—a system tangibly represented by a tripartite division of settlement size, that is, hamlets, villages, and populous centers and the construction of monumental public works. A closer look will, perhaps, provide us a developmental perspective on these issues.

There can be little doubt that the social core of ancient Mississippian communities was an aggregate of consanguineal kinsmen (Peebles 1974). That is, each community contained a network of interlocking parent-child and sibling ties that served as the social charter for distributing rights and duties, privileges and obligations, but the archaeological evidence at hand seems to indicate that not all parent-child and sibling bonds were of equal value. After death, some Mississippians were interred in temple mounds, or other special places, and were accompanied by sumptuous grave goods. Others were buried beneath their houses or in cemeteries and were accompanied by a far more modest supply of grave goods or no grave goods at all (Peebles 1974). The differential treatment accorded the dead may be interpreted in two ways: (1) as indicating inequalities of rank within the society at large or (2) as signaling the rank of the deceased. The first interpretation merely states that some members of a Mississippian community were set apart from others by virtue of their birth and/or personal accomplishments and may have constituted an indigenous, if nascent, aristocracy. The second holds that the rank indicated is that of the deceased. Thus, if lavish burial treatment is given an infant, we may infer ascribed status. From this second perspective, children of high-status persons, by virtue of birth alone, were expected to assume positions of power and prestige with little, if any, need to validate them by personal effort or initiative.

The first interpretation is the more cautious and fits the pattern of native American status striving a bit better than the second. Throughout much of native North America, status was achieved, or enhanced, by the distribution or destruction of wealth rather than by its accumulation. This distribution or destruction often took place at group ceremonials, burial among them. Hence, the wealth included with an infant burial might mark the status-striving efforts of a living relative, rather than the rank of the deceased. We are not arguing that this is invariably the case, only that it could be; it must be discounted if more elaborate interpretive edifices are to be built on the analysis of burial practices. At any rate, the basis for inequality of rank in Mississippian societies needs further attention.

Let us take the more cautious view and assume that ranking was a product of genealogical position that required validation through personal accomplishment. In other words, let us assume that the number of parent-offspring and sibling links to a high-ranking ancestor could be used to claim a particular rank if and when warranted by personal achievements. In such a system, the fewer the links to a ranking ancestor, the higher the rank that could be claimed. Lineal links should, however, be distinguished from collateral links. The former are to be construed as any concatenation of parent-child ties. The latter are sibling ties in any biological generation other than one's own. Thus, two lineal links connect a person to his grandfather (fa, fa) and one lineal and one collateral link connect any person to his father's brother (fa, bro). Now, if we can assume primogeniture in calculating the genealogical links from ego to an ancestor, any chain of kin ties that includes a collateral link will be longer than one that includes only lineal links.

In kin groups of the kind being considered, there will always be far fewer lineals than collaterals. As a given population grows, the number of people who must count a collateral link to claim descent from a common ancestor will increase far faster than the number able to trace the relationship through lineal links alone. For example, let us assume a common ancestor who produces two offspring, each of whom produces two offspring and so on. After four generations, 4 descendants will be able to count lineal links, 12 must include collateral ties. After eight generations still only 4 descendants will be able to count lineal links alone, whereas 252 must include collateral ties. If access to status and prestige were to be justified by such a genealogical net, and in the manner described, then the potential for seeking community rewards might be characterized as flowing downward from ancestor to descendants and outward from higher-ranking lineal to lower-ranking collateral kinsmen. In sum, we suspect that a few members of any descent group had, by reason of their accomplishments and genealogical position, the right to decide what goals were desirable and to direct the attention and labor of other descent-group members toward attaining them. One of these goals, we think, was temple and mound building.

The effort and attention given to mounds were, in part, consequences of the complex body of esoteric knowledge that shaped Mississippian ceremonialism. One of the objectives of Mississippian ritualism was, it seems, world renewal. World renewal was expressed through mound purification, that is, the periodic modification of mound surfaces with a blanket of ashes and sanctified earth (see Schnell, Knight, and Schnell 1981) and through maize ceremonialism, which according to Howard (1968, 80–88) had four parts: (1) the extinguishing of the old year's fire, (2) the making of the new year's fire, (3) the expiation of the past year's sins (murder excepted), and (4) the communal eating of the new maize. These four steps can be understood as symbolic statements of purification and growth which were integrated with mound modification as follows. The fireplace ash and dirt from cleaning and purifying socially important public and perhaps private places (plazas, dancing grounds, and houses) when ritually treated provided the raw material for annual mound enlargement. Hence, mound renewal incorporated the purified detritus of the past year's sins, removed it from the realm of the profane, and made it into the sacred surface upon which the future was to be built. Thus, as maize eating and the expiation of sins led to physical and spiritual growth for the individual, the mound's ritual consumption of the detritus of past sins led to its growth as a physical and presumably a spiritual entity. Be this as it may, mounds also grew through major rebuilding episodes. These seem to have accompanied the death of an authority. With the destruction of his mound-top temple/dwelling and his burial beneath its floor, the mound was converted to a tomb. With its subsequent enlargement, the mound became a funerary monument as well as a temple mound. In its mortuary function a temple mound was like its Hopewell predecessor—an elaborate stage setting for public burial rites, except that in the Mississippian case, only the remains of a select few would be so honored (see Schnell, Knight, and Schnell 1981, 141–45).

Thus, temple mounds may have played a dual social role. On the one hand they were tangible representations of the right to legitimate exercise of power and authority by a select few. On the other, they purified the community, sanctified it, and represented its wealth, glory, and capability as well. Hence, some Mississippian mounds may be considered both public and private monuments. They were both community shrines (perhaps dedicated to gods) and markers of a cardinal social principle (symbols of ranking). Then, too, Mississippian mounds grew through annual enlargement and episodic rebuilding, both of which required massed manpower—manpower thus committed to the authority the mounds represented. Working toward a common ritual goal promoted worker solidarity while it provided spiritual and material rewards. In the case at hand, these rewards took the tangible form of a monument and the intangible form of civic pride and a community fund of prestige in which all might share, albeit differentially. There were, however, limits to the rewards that could be adequately distributed and the authority that could be maintained through mound building.

It has been noted that lineals could claim the greatest share of a monument's prestige yield, near collaterals could claim less, distant collaterals still less. Yet even the most distant collaterals must have provided construction labor. The disparity between labor owed and rewards received would have grown as group size increased and the kin and social gulf between lineals and collaterals widened. Thus, there would have come a time in the group's growth when the vast majority of members were only distantly related to its leaders. They could, therefore, claim but little of the glory and power these authorities represented. When this happened, resentments could have resulted, and dissatisfied portions of the population might have begun to question traditionally held assumptions about the legitimate transfer and use of power. These dissidents would have formed a potential body of followers should disputes over succession to status or title have emerged among competing descent group members claiming higher rank.

The available ethnographic evidence indicates that in unilateral descent groups, disputes over succession to status or title occur most frequently among half brothers, that is, a high-ranking man's descendants by separate wives (Service 1975, 78). Each of the descendants has a claim (although some claims may be stronger than others) and each may call upon his non-descent-related relatives for support, that is, may use the affiliative bond noted earlier. As the struggle over leadership unfolds, the number and disposition of each competitor's relatives may play an important role. Nevertheless, only one competitor can win. Each loser, however, has identified himself as a potential leader and a potential threat to the established order. Such a man may become the focal point for other dissidents, who see in him a means for advancing their own cause. Thus, a claimant to title and high status, though unsuccessful, may attract a sufficient number of determined followers among his own kinsmen and other dissatisfied segments of the population to set himself up as an authority should he so choose.

After identifying a willing body of relatives and other followers for his support, a potential authority may consider several possible moves. If his challenge has created bitterness and suspicion, he may choose to found an independent settlement. Conditions for such a move must, however, be right. There must be suitable land available beyond the parent community's reach. Then, too, founding a totally independent settlement requires a following of sufficient size and vigor to provide for the common defense and achieve economic security. If conditions for founding an independent community are not right and there is suitable space available in the parent community's hinterland, the dissident authority may found a colony that retains social, ceremonial, and economic ties to its parent while establishing an independent or pseudo-independent local authority structure. Finally, if suitable hinterland space is not available, or if the military and/or economic risks of removal are prohibitive, the potential leader may choose to remain within the parent community and seek other means to promote recognition of his claims. By carefully manipulating affinal alliances and kin ties, through success in war, trade, and other economic enterprises, a shrewd potential leader might marshal the wealth and support necessary to further his own ambitions. If these ethnographic considerations can be applied to the political process in Mississippian communities, they might shed new light on some mound-building practices. For example, an emergent Mississippian leader, whether resident, colonist, or independent migrant, might have advanced his cause and consolidated his position by building a mound for his ancestors, his followers, his descendants, and especially for himself.

This admittedly speculative model for the Mississippian political process could account for two infrequently discussed aspects of temple mound building. The first of these is the occurrence of numerous multimound settlements. If temple mound building had the social significance and solidarity-promoting effects envisioned, multiple contemporary mounds are the predictable consequence of population growth and competition for status and prestige in favorably located and politically mature settlements. Moreover, the propensity to rebuild, refurbish, and enlarge existing temple mounds, behavior often relegated to religious fervor, assumes new meaning. Major rebuilding and enlargement in this model reflect succession to leadership. In other words, changes of leadership that accompany the death or removal of an authority are marked by the beginning of a major new temple mound construction episode. From this point of view some Mississippian mound building chronicles succession to office and title as well as it does ritual purification. The model contains other developmental implications that also bear discussion.

By A.D. 900, population growth and the narrowing of the resource range had led to the creation of farming communities with authority and prestige distribution practices centered on the construction and maintenance of earthen temple-tombs. Between A.D. 900 and 1400, the authority and prestige distribution limits inhering in mound building and other public works programs worked together with continued population growth to produce a dispersed pattern of populous centers, satellite communities, hamlets, and homesteads (see Smith 1978). Internal ranking both created these developments and accompanied them as opposition between original settlers and newcomers, senior and junior descent lines, those rising to prominence and those in decline, hardened into a locally and regionally stratified social order. Once maturity was achieved, modifications of the social order could be attained through demographic growth or decline; successful or unsuccessful management of resources, people, or alliances; and victory or defeat in warfare.

Successful competitors might, for instance, translate otherwise temporary social gains into genealogical claims with modified pedigrees to back them up, but there was a limit to the growth that could be thus sustained. As a chief or other leader drew a greater following through judicious management, he reached a point at which his radius of action was easily checked by ambitious kinsmen and their allies who were protecting their own interests. By virtue of a competitor's growth, an ambitious yet less powerful authority could, for a while at least, offer greater immediate returns. Thus, centers of power and prestige as they grew larger spawned their own competitors and by virtue of their growth yielded the advantage to them. To supersede the limitations of a monument-based prestige yield system and the kin order which it exemplified, an authority had to gain independent access to reliable and renewable resources of his own. One means to this end was control of commerce, and some of the populous late Mississippian communities were participating in a moderate commerce which may have promoted a tendency toward craft specialization and other forms of entrepreneurship.

Greater commercial prosperity might have ultimately broadened the base provided by traditional forms of prestige distribution and temporarily, at least, allowed entrenched authorities to control a larger following. Indeed, if commerce had expanded further, Mississippian communities might have moved toward those forms of sociocultural integration that promote the formation of states. But without external forms of wealth in sufficient volume, there were real limits to the population that could be controlled by traditional means. Lacking a substantial and renewable external form of wealth, Mississippian societies would be forced to depend upon the management of locally available resources which would limit the economic growth their technology could sustain. Ultimately, continued population growth would combine with limited economic potentials, intensified intra- and inter-group competition, and ecological mismanagement or stress to produce severe strains in the fabric of Mississippian society.

In the fifteenth century, for instance, here faster, there slower, the more elaborate expressions of mound building and other public works were discontinued (Sheldon 1974). We may presume that the organizing social and political force behind them had, in part at least, collapsed (Peebles 1970). In sum, Mississippian sociopolitical organization contained the seeds of its own destruction, namely the prestige distribution limits inhering in monument building as a vehicle for expressing and maintaining authority. Our model of the Mississippian political process, should it prove tenable, would therefore be consonant with the view that the protohistoric simplification of social, political, and economic life did indeed represent a waning of momentum, a dissipation of organizational force, which, without the intercession of additional and most probably external pressures, could not have been reformulated to the end of state and empire building.

References Cited

Antevs, E.
  1955 Geologic-Climatic Dating in the West. *American Antiquity* 20:317–35.
Atkins, S., and J. MacMahan
  1967 The Zabski Site Merritt Island, Florida. *Florida Anthropologist* 20:133–45.
Atkinson, J.
  1978 A Cultural Resources Survey of Selected Construction Areas in the Tennessee-Tombigbee Waterway: Alabama and Mississippi I. Report on file. Starkville: Department of Anthropology, Mississippi State University.
Atkinson, J., J. Phillips, and R. Walling
  1980 *The Kellogg Village Site Investigations, Clay County, Mississippi.* Starkville: Department of Anthropology, Mississippi State University.
Beardsley, R., P. Holder, A. Krieger, B. Meggers, J. Rinaldo, and P. Kutsche
  1956 Functional and Evolutionary Implications of Community Patterning. In R. Wauchope, ed., *Seminars in Archaeology.* Memoir 11. Salt Lake City: Society for American Archaeology.
Binford, L.
  1962 Archaeology as Anthropology. *American Antiquity* 28:217–25.
  1965 Archaeological Systematics and the Study of Cultural Process. *American Antiquity* 31:203–10.
Blakeman, C.
  1975 Archaeological Investigations in the Upper Central Tombigbee Valley: 1974 Season. Report on file. Starkville: Department of Anthropology, Mississippi State University.
  1976 A Cultural Resource Survey of the Aberdeen Lock and Dam and Canal Section Areas of the Tennessee-Tombigbee Waterway: 1975. Report on file. Starkville: Department of Anthropology, Mississippi State University.
Boas, F.
  1948 *Race, Language and Culture.* New York: Macmillan.

Bohannon, C.
  1972   Excavations at the Pharr Mounds: Prentiss and Itawamba Counties, Mis-
         sissippi and Excavations at the Bear Creek Site; Tishomingo County, Mis-
         sissippi. Report on file. Washington, D.C.: National Park Service, Office of
         Archeology and Historic Preservation.
Brasher, T.
  1973   An Investigation of Some Central Functions of Poverty Point. Master's the-
         sis, Northwestern State University of Louisiana.
Brose, D., N. Jenkins, and R. Weisman
  1982   An Archaeological Reconnaissance of the Black Warrior/Lower Tombigbee
         Valley and Mobile Delta, Alabama. Report on file. Mobile: Department of
         Geography and Geology, University of South Alabama.
Broster, J.
  1975   Preliminary Report of the Pinson Mounds Project, 1974. Nashville: Division
         of Archaeology, Tennessee Department of Conservation.
Broster, J., and L. Schneider
  1975   *The Pinson Mounds Archaeology Project: Excavation of 1974 and 1975.*
         Research Series 1. Nashville: Division of Archaeology, Tennessee Depart-
         ment of Conservation.
Brown, J.
  1976   The Southern Cult Revisited. *Mid-Continental Journal of Archaeology*
         11(2):115–36.
  1979   Charnel Houses and Mortuary Crypts: Disposal of the Dead in the Middle
         Woodland Period. In D. Brose and N. Greber, eds., *Hopewell Archaeology:
         The Chillicothe Conference.* Kent: Kent State University Press.
Buikstra, J.
  1976   *Hopewell in the Lower Illinois Valley: A Regional Study of Human Biolog-
         ical Variability and Prehistoric Mortuary Behavior.* Archaeological Program
         Scientific Papers 2. Evanston: Northwestern University.
Bullen, R.
  1959   The Transitional Period of Florida. *Southeastern Archaeological Con-
         ference, Newsletter* 6:43–53.
  1966   Stela at the Crystal River Site, Florida. *American Antiquity* 31:861–65.
  1969   Excavations at Sunday Bluff, Florida. *Contributions of the Florida State
         Museum. Social Sciences* 15. Gainesville.
  1972   The Orange Period of Peninsular Florida. In R. Bullen and J. Stoltman, eds.,
         Fiber-Tempered Pottery in the Southeastern United States and Northern Co-
         lumbia: Its Origins, Context, and Significance. *Florida Anthropologist*
         25(2):9–33.
Bullen, R., and A. Bullen
  1961   The Summer Haven Site, St. Johns County, Florida. *Florida Anthropologist*
         14(1–2):1–15.
Caddell, G.
  1981a Plant Resources, Archaeological Plant Remains, and Prehistoric Plant-Use
         Patterns in the Central Tombigbee River Valley. In *Biocultural Studies in the
         Gainesville Lake Area of the Tennessee-Tombigbee Waterway.* Vol. 4. Report

of Investigations 14. University: Office of Archaeological Research, University of Alabama.

1981b Floral Remains from the Lubbub Creek Archaeological Locality. In C. Peebles, ed., Studies of the Material Remains from the Lubbub Creek Archaeological Locality: Prehistoric Agricultural Communities in West Central Alabama. Vol. 2. Report on file. Ann Arbor: Museum of Anthropology, University of Michigan.

Caldwell, J.

1958 *Trend and Tradition in the Prehistory of the Eastern United States.* Memoir 88. Springfield: American Anthropological Association.

1964 Interaction Spheres in Prehistory. In J. Caldwell and R. Hall, eds., *Hopewellian Studies.* Scientific Papers 12. Springfield: Illinois State Museum.

Carneiro, R.

1970 A Theory of the Origin of the State. *Science* 169:733–38.

Champe, J.

1946 *Ash Hollow Cave.* University of Nebraska Studies no. 1. Lincoln.

Chase, D.

1972 Evidence of Bayou La Batre-Archaic Contact. *Journal of Alabama Archaeology* 18(2):151–61.

Clarke, D.

1968 *Analytical Archaeology.* London: Methuen.

Coe, M.

1962 *Mexico.* New York: Praeger.

1966 *The Maya.* New York: Praeger.

Cole, G., and C. Albright

1981 Summerville I-II Fortifications. In C. Peebles, ed., Excavations in the Lubbub Creek Archaeological Locality: Prehistoric Agricultural Communities in West Central Alabama. Vol. 1. Report on file. Ann Arbor: Museum of Anthropology, University of Michigan.

Connaway, J., and S. McGahey

1971 *Archaeological Excavation at the Boyd Site, Tunica County, Mississippi.* Technical Reports 1. Jackson, Miss.: Department of Archives and History.

Connaway, J., S. McGahey, and C. Webb

1977 *Teoc Creek: A Poverty Point Site in Carroll County, Mississippi.* Archaeological Report 3. Jackson, Miss.: Department of Archives and History.

Cotter, J.

1937 The Occurrence of Flints and Extinct Animals in Pluvial Deposits Near Clovis, New Mexico. *Proceedings of the Academy of Natural Sciences of Philadelphia* 89:1–16.

Cotter, J., and J. Corbett

1951 *Archeology of the Bynum Mounds, Mississippi.* Archeological Research Series 1. Washington, D.C.: National Park Service.

Crane, H., and J. Griffin

1959 University of Michigan Radiocarbon Dates IV. *American Journal of Science Radiocarbon Supplement* 1:173–98.

Daniel, G.
   1967   *The Origins and Growth of Archaeology.* New York: Crowell.
Deetz, J.
   1965   *The Dynamics of Stylistic Change in Arikara Ceramics.* Illinois Studies in
          Anthropology 4. Urbana: University of Illinois Press.
Deevey, E., and R. Flint
   1957   Postglacial Hypsithermal Interval. *Science* 125:3240.
DeJarnette, D., J. Walthall, and S. Wimberly
   1975   Archaeological Investigations in the Buttahatchee River Valley, Lamar
          County, Alabama. *Journal of Alabama Archaeology* 21(1):1–37.
DePratter, C.
   1975   The Archaic in Georgia. *Early Georgia* 3(1):1–16.
Dixon, R.
   1913   Some Aspects of North American Archaeology. *American Anthropologist*
          15:549–77.
Drucker, P., R. Heizer, and R. Squier
   1959   Excavations at LaVenta Tabasco, 1955. Bulletin 170. Washington, D.C.:
          Bureau of American Ethnology.
Dunnell, R.
   1971   *Systematics in Prehistory.* New York: Free Press.
Dye, D.
   1980   Primary Forest Efficiency in the Western Middle Tennessee Valley. Ph.D.
          diss., Department of Anthropology, Washington University.
Ensor, B.
   1980   An Evaluation and Synthesis of Changing Lithic Technologies in the Central
          Tombigbee Valley. *Southeastern Archaeological Conference Bulletin* 22:83–
          90.
   1981   Classification and Synthesis of the Gainesville Lake Area Lithic Materials:
          Chronology, Technology and Use. In *Archaeological Investigations in the
          Gainesville Lake Area of the Tennessee-Tombigbee Waterway.* Vol. 3. Report
          of Investigations 13. University: Office of Archaeological Research, Univer-
          sity of Alabama.
Fagan, B.
   1980   *People of the Earth.* 3d ed. Boston: Little, Brown.
Fairbanks, C.
   1942   The Taxonomic Position of Stalling's Island, Georgia. *American Antiquity*
          7:223–31.
Faulkner, C.
   1971   The Mississippian-Woodland Transition in the Middle South. Paper present-
          ed at the 29th Southeastern Archaeological Conference, Macon, Ga.
Faulkner, C., and J. B. Graham
   1966   Westmoreland-Barber Site (40Mi-11) Nickajack Reservoir: Season II. Re-
          port on file. Knoxville: Department of Anthropology, University of
          Tennessee.
Faulkner, C., and C. R. McCollough
   1974   Excavation and Testing, Normandy Reservoir Salvage Project: 1972 Season,

Normandy Archaeological Project. Vol. 2. Report of Investigations 12. Knoxville: Department of Anthropology, University of Tennessee.

Fisher, F., and C. McNutt
   1962   Test Excavations at Pinson Mounds, 1961. *Tennessee Archaeologist* 18 (1):1–13.

Flannery, K.
   1968a Archaeological Systems Theory and Early Mesoamerica. In B. Meggers, ed., *Anthropological Archaeology in the Americas*. Washington, D.C.: Anthropological Society of Washington.
   1968b The Olmec and the Valley of the Oaxaca. Washington, D.C.: Dumbarton Oaks Conference on the Olmec, 79–110.

Flint, R.
   1947   *Glacial Geology and the Pleistocene Epoch*. New York: Wiley.

Ford, J.
   1936   *Analysis of Indian Village Site Collections from Louisiana and Mississippi*. Anthropological Study no. 2. New Orleans: Louisiana Geological Survey.
   1952   *Measurements of Some Prehistoric Design Developments in the Southeastern States*. Anthropological Papers 44(3). New York: American Museum of Natural History.

Ford, J., and G. Quimby
   1945   *The Tchefuncte Culture, An Early Occupation of the Lower Mississippi Valley*. Memoir 2. Menasha: Society for American Archaeology.

Ford, J., and C. Webb
   1956   *Poverty Point, A Late Archaic Site in Louisiana*. Anthropological Papers 46. New York: American Museum of Natural History.

Ford, J., and G. Willey
   1940   *Crooks Site, A Marksville Period Burial Mound in LaSalle Parish, Louisiana*. Anthropology Study 3. New Orleans: Louisiana Geological Survey.

Fortes, M.
   1953   The Structure of Unilineal Descent Groups. *American Anthropologist* 55:17–41.

Gagliano, S., and C. Webb
   1970   Archaic-Poverty Point Transition at the Pearl River Mouth. *Southeastern Archaeological Conference Bulletin* 12:47–72.

Gibbon, G.
   1974   A Model of Mississippian Development and Its Implications for the Red Wing Area. In E. Johnson, ed., *Aspects of Upper Great Lakes Anthropology*. Saint Paul: Minnesota Historical Society.

Gibson, J.
   1973   Social Systems at Poverty Point: An Analysis of Intersite and Intrasite Variability. Ph.D. diss., Southern Methodist University.
   1974   Poverty Point: The First North American Chiefdom. *Archaeology* 27(2):97–105.
   1979   Poverty Point Trade in South Central Louisiana: An Illustration from Beau Rivage. *Louisiana Archaeology* 4:91–116.

Gilder, R.
  1907 The Nebraska Loess Man. *Records of the Past* 6(2):35–39.
  1926 *The Nebraska Culture Man.* Omaha: H. R. Kieser.
Goggin, J.
  1949 Culture Traditions in Florida Prehistory. In J. W. Griffin, ed., *The Florida Indian and His Neighbors.* Winter Park, Fla.: Rollins College.
Goodenough, W.
  1970 *Description and Comparison in Cultural Anthropology.* Chicago: Aldine.
Griffin, J.
  1946 Cultural Change and Continuity in Eastern United States Archaeology. Man in Northeastern North America. Papers of the Robert S. Peabody Foundation for Archaeology, 3. Andover.
Griffin, J., ed.
  1952a *Archeology of the Eastern United States.* Chicago: University of Chicago Press.
  1952b Some Early and Middle Woodland Pottery Types in Illinois. In T. Deuel, ed., *Hopewellian Communities in Illinois.* Scientific Papers 5. Springfield: Illinois State Museum.
  1966 Mesoamerica and the Eastern United States in Prehistoric Times. In G. Ekholm and G. Willey, eds., *Archaeological Frontiers and External Connections, Handbook of Middle American Indians.* Vol. 4. Tulane University: Middle American Research Institute.
  1967 Eastern North American Archaeology: A Summary. *Science* 156:175–91.
  1985 Changing Concepts of the Prehistoric Mississippian Cultures of the Eastern United States. In R. Badger and L. Clayton, eds., *Alabama and the Borderlands: From Prehistory to Statehood.* University: University of Alabama Press.
Griffin, J. W., and H. Smith
  1954 *The Cotton Site: An Archaeological Site of Early Ceramic Times in Volusia County, Florida.* Florida State University Studies 16. Tallahassee.
Haag, W.
  1939 Pottery Type Descriptions. *Southeastern Archaeological Newsletter* 1(1).
  1942 A Description of Analysis of the Pickwick Basin Pottery. In W. Webb and D. DeJarnette, eds., *An Archaeological Survey of Pickwick Basin in the Adjacent Portions of the States of Alabama, Mississippi, and Tennessee.* Bulletin 129. Washington, D.C.: Bureau of American Ethnology.
Hammond, N.
  1977 The Earliest Maya. *Scientific American* 236:116–23.
Hardin, M.
  1980 The Recognition of Individual Hands in the Context of Standardized Craft Production: Implications of the Technological and Stylistic Development of Moundville Engraved Ceramics. *Southeastern Archaeological Conference Bulletin* 24:18–29.
Harris, M.
  1968 *The Rise of Anthropological Theory.* New York: Crowell.

Haury, E.
   1953   Artifacts with Mammoth Remains, Naco, Arizona. *American Antiquity* 19:1–14.
Heimlich, M.
   1952   *Guntersville Basin Pottery*. Museum Paper 32. University: Geological Survey of Alabama.
Hester, J., and J. Grady
   1982   *Introduction to Archaeology*. 2d ed. New York: Holt, Rinehart and Winston.
Hill, M.
   1981   Analysis, Synthesis and Interpretation of the Skeletal Material Excavated for the Gainesville Section of the Tennessee-Tombigbee Waterway. In *Biocultural Studies in the Gainesville Lake Area of the Tennessee-Tombigbee Waterway*. Vol. 4. Report of Investigations 14. University: Office of Archaeological Research, University of Alabama.
Holder, P.
   1970   *The Hoe and the Horse on the Plains: A Study of Cultural Development among North American Indians*. Lincoln: University of Nebraska Press.
Holmes, G.
   1914   Areas of American Cultural Characterization Tentatively Outlined as an Aid in the Study of Antiquities. *American Anthropologist* 16:13–16.
Howard, J.
   1968   *The Southeastern Ceremonial Complex and Its Interpretation*. Memoir 6. Columbia: Missouri Archaeological Society.
Hubbert, C.
   1978   *A Cultural Resource Survey of the Bay Springs Segment of the Tennessee-Tombigbee Waterway*. Report of Investigations 3. University: Office of Archaeological Research, University of Alabama.
Hurt, W.
   1953   Report of the Investigation of the Thomas Riggs Site, 39Hu1, Hughes County, South Dakota, 1952. Archaeological Studies 5. Vermillion: University of South Dakota.
Jenkins, N.
   1972   A Fiber Tempered Vessel from the Tombigbee Basin. *Journal of Alabama Archaeology* 18(2):162–66.
   1975a Archaeological Investigations in the Gainesville Lock and Dam Reservoir: 1974. Report on file. University: Department of Anthropology, University of Alabama.
   1975b The Wheeler Series and Southeastern Prehistory. *Florida Anthropologist* 18:17–26.
   1976   Terminal Woodland-Mississippian Interaction in Northern Alabama: The West Jefferson Phase. Paper presented at the 33d Annual Meeting of the Southeastern Archaeological Conference, Tuscaloosa.
   1979   Miller Hopewell of the Tombigbee Drainage. In D. Brose and N. Greber, eds., *Hopewell Archaeology: The Chillicothe Conference*. Kent: Kent State University Press.

1981 Gainesville Lake Area Ceramic Description and Chronology. In *Archaeological Investigations in the Gainesville Lake Area of the Tennessee-Tombigbee Waterway.* Vol. 2. Report of Investigations 12. University: Office of Archaeological Research, University of Alabama.

1982 Archaeology of the Gainesville Lake Area: Synthesis. In *Archaeological Investigations in the Gainesville Lake Area of the Tennessee-Tombigbee Waterway.* Vol. 5. Report of Investigations 23. University: Office of Archaeological Research, University of Alabama.

Jenkins, N., C. Curren, and M. DeLeon
1975 *Archaeological Site Survey of the Demopolis and Gainesville Lake Navigation Channels and Additional Construction Areas.* Report on file. University: Department of Anthropology, University of Alabama.

Jenkins, N., and H. Ensor
1981 The Gainesville Lake Area Excavations. In *Archaeological Investigations in the Gainesville Lake Area of the Tennessee-Tombigbee Waterway.* Vol. 1. Report of Investigations 11. University: Office of Archaeological Research, University of Alabama.

Jenkins, N., and J. Nielsen
1974 Archaeological Salvage Investigations at the West Jefferson Steam Plant Site, Jefferson County, Alabama. Report on file. Moundville: Mound State Monument.

Jennings, J.
1941 Chickasaw and Earlier Cultures of Northwest Mississippi. *Journal of Mississippi History* 3(3):155–226.

1944 The Archaeological Survey of the Natchez Trace. *American Antiquity* 4:408–14.

1974 *Prehistory of North America.* New York: McGraw-Hill.

Johnston, R.
1968 *The Archaeology of the Serpent Mounds Site.* Occasional Papers 10. Ontario: Art and Archaeology Division, Royal Ontario Museum.

Kay, P.
1971 Taxonomy and Semantic Contrast. *Language* 47(4):866–86.

Kidder, A. V.
1924 *An Introduction to the Study of Southwestern Archaeology.* New Haven: Yale University Press.

1968 *An Introduction to the Study of Southwestern Archaeology with a Preliminary Account of the Excavations at Pecos.* New Haven: Yale University Press.

Knight, V.
1981 Mississippian Ritual. Ph.D. diss., Anthropology Department, University of Florida.

Koehler, T.
1966 *Archaeological Excavation of the Womack Mound (22-Ya-1).* Bulletin 1. University: Mississippi Archaeological Association.

Krause, R.
1967 Arikara Ceramic Change: A Study of the Factors Affecting Stylistic Change

in Late 18th and Early 19th Century Arikara Pottery. Ph.D. diss., Department of Anthropology, Yale University.

1970   Aspects of Adaptation among Upper Republican Subsistence Cultivators. In W. Dort and J. Jones, eds., *Pleistocene and Recent Environments of the Central Great Plains*. Special Publication 3. Lawrence: University of Kansas.

1977   Taxonomic Practice and Middle Missouri Prehistory: A Perspective on Donald J. Lehmer's Contributions. In W. Wood, ed., *Plains Anthropologist, Memoir* 13:5–14.

Krieger, A.

1953   New World Culture History: Anglo-America. In A. L. Kroeber, ed., *Anthropology Today*. Chicago: University of Chicago Press.

Kroeber, A. L.

1931   The Culture-Area and Age-Area Concepts of Clark Wissler. In S. Rice, ed., *Methods in Social Science*. Chicago: University of Chicago Press.

1939   *Cultural and Natural Areas of Native North America*. Publications in American Archaeology and Ethnology 38. Berkeley: University of California.

Kroeber, A. L., and H. Driver

1932   *Quantificative Expression of Cultural Relationships*. Publications in American Archaeology and Ethnology 29. Berkeley: University of California.

Kushner, G.

1970   A Consideration of Some Processual Designs for Archaeology as Anthropology. *American Antiquity* 35:125–32.

Lafferty, R.

1973   An Analysis of Prehistoric Southeastern Fortifications. Master's thesis, Department of Anthropology, Southern Illinois University.

Larson, L.

1972   Functional Considerations of Warfare in the Southeast during the Mississippi Period. *American Antiquity* 37:383–92.

Lazarus, W.

1965   Alligator Lake, a Ceramic Horizon on the Northwest Florida Coast. *Florida Anthropologist* 1:83–124.

Leach, E.

1961   *Rethinking Anthropology*. London School of Economics Monographs on Social Anthropology 22. London: Athlong Press.

Leacock, E.

1963   Introduction to *Ancient Society*. New York: Meridian Books.

Lehmer, D.

1970   Climate and Culture History in the Middle Missouri Valley. In W. Dort and J. Jones, eds., *Pleistocene and Recent Environments of the Central Great Plains*. Special Publication 3. Lawrence: University of Kansas.

1971   *Introduction to Middle Missouri Archeology*. Anthropological Papers 1. Washington, D.C.: National Park Service.

Lewis, R.

1974   *Mississippian Exploitative Strategies: A Southeast Missouri Example*. Research Series 11. Columbia: Missouri Archaeology Society.

Lewis, T.
  1954 A Suggested Basis for Paleo-Indian Chronology in Tennessee and the East-
        ern United States. *Southern Indian Studies* 5:11–13.
Linné, S.
  1934 *Archaeological Researches at Teotihuacan, Mexico.* Stockholm: Ethno-
        graphical Museum of Sweden.
Longacre, W.
  1970 *Archaeology as Anthropology: A Case Study.* Anthropological Papers 17.
        Tucson: University of Arizona.
McGee, W. J., and C. Thomas
  1905 Prehistoric North America. In F. N. Thorpe, ed., *The History of North
        America.* Vol. 19. Philadelphia: George Barree.
McKern, W.
  1939 The Midwestern Taxonomic Method as an Aid to Archaeological Culture
        Study. *American Antiquity* 4:301–13.
MacNeish, R.
  1964a The Origins of New World Civilization. *Scientific American* 211(5):29–37.
  1964b Ancient Mesoamerican Civilization. *Science* 143:531–37.
  1967 *The Prehistory of the Tehuacan Valley.* Vol. 2: *The Nonceramic Artifacts.*
        Austin: University of Texas Press.
  1971 Early Man in the Andes. *Scientific American* 224(4):36–46.
Mainfort, R.
  1980 *Archaeological Investigations at Pinson Mounds State Archaelogical Area:
        1974, 1975, 1978 Field Seasons.* Research Series 1. Nashville: Division of
        Archaeology, Tennessee Department of Conservation.
Marshall, R.
  1977 Lyon's Bluff Site (220K1) Radiocarbon Dated. *Journal of Alabama Archae-
        ology* 23(1):53–57.
Marx, K.
  1977 *Capital: A Critique of Political Economy.* Vol. 1. Trans. B. Fowkes. New
        York: Random House, Vintage Books. (First published in German, 1867.)
Mason, O. T.
  1896 Influence of Environment upon Human Industries or Arts. In *Smithsonian
        Institution, Annual Report for 1895.* Washington, D.C.
Meyer, W.
  1922 Archaeological Fieldwork in South Dakota and Missouri. *Smithsonian Mis-
        cellaneous Collections* 72(15):117–25.
Millon, R.
  1970 Teotihuacán: Completion of Map of Giant Ancient City in the Valley of
        Mexico. *Science* 170:1077–82.
Moore, C.
  1901 Certain Aboriginal Remains of the Tombigbee River. *Journal of the Acade-
        my of Natural Sciences of Philadelphia* 11(4):289–337.
  1905 Certain Aboriginal Remains of the Lower Tombigbee River. *Journal of the
        Academy of Natural Sciences of Philadelphia* 13(2):245–78.

Morgan, Lewis H.
  1877 *Ancient Society.* New York: World Publishing.
Morse, D., and J. Polhemus
  n.d.(a) Preliminary Investigations of the Pinson Mounds Site Near Jackson, Tennessee. Report on file. Nashville: Division of Archaeology, Tennessee Department of Conservation.
  n.d.(b) Archaeological Field Investigations in the Cordell Hill Reservoir, Tennessee: 1963 Field Season. Report on file. Fayetteville: Arkansas Archaeological Survey.
Mott, Mildred
  1938 The Relation of Historic Indian Tribes to Archaeological Manifestations in Iowa. *Iowa Journal of History and Politics* 36(3):207–304.
Murdock, G.
  1949 *Social Structure.* New York: Macmillan.
Myer, W.
  1922 Recent Archaeological Discoveries in Tennessee. *Art and Archaeology* 14:140–50.
  1928 *Indian Trails of the Southeast.* Annual Report 42. Washington, D.C.: Bureau of American Ethnology.
Netting, R.
  1965 A Trial Model of Cultural Ecology. *Anthropological Quarterly* 38:81–95.
O'Hear, J., C. Larsen, M. Scarry, J. Phillips, and E. Simons
  1981 Archaeological Salvage Excavations at the Tibbee Creek Site (22Lo600) Lowndes County, Mississippi. Report on file. Starkville: Department of Anthropology, Mississippi State University.
Peebles, C.
  1970 Moundville and Beyond: Some Observations on the Changing Social Organization in the Southeastern United States. Paper presented at the 69th Annual Meeting of the American Anthropological Association, San Diego.
  1974 Moundville: The Organization of a Prehistoric Community and Culture. Ph.D. diss., Department of Anthropology, University of California, Santa Barbara.
  1978 Determinants of Settlement Size and Location in the Moundville Phase. In B. D. Smith, ed., *Mississippian Settlement Patterns.* New York: Academic Press.
Peebles, C., ed.
  1981 Excavations in the Lubbub Creek Archaeological Locality: Prehistoric Agricultural Communities in West Central Alabama. Vol. 1. Report on file. Ann Arbor: Museum of Anthropology, University of Michigan.
Peebles, C., and J. Blitz
  1981 The Summerville II and III Community. In C. Peebles, ed., Excavations in the Lubbub Creek Archaeological Locality: Prehistoric Agricultural Communities in West Central Alabama. Vol. 1. Report on file. Ann Arbor: Museum of Anthropology, University of Michigan.

Peebles, C., and S. Kus
   1977   Some Archaeological Correlates of Ranked Societies. *American Antiquity*
          42:421–49.
Peebles, C., and C. Mann
   1981   A Chronological Seriation of the Mississippian Ceramics from the Lubbub
          Creek Archaeological Locality. In C. Peebles, ed., Excavations in the Lub-
          bub Creek Archaeological Locality: Prehistoric Agricultural Communities in
          West Central Alabama. Vol. 1. Report on file. Ann Arbor: Museum of An-
          thropology, University of Michigan.
Penman, J.
   1977   *Archaeological Survey in Mississippi.* Archaeological Report 2. Jackson,
          Miss.: Department of Archives and History.
Peterson, D.
   1970   The Refuge Phase in the Savannah River Region. *Southeastern Archae-
          ological Conference Bulletin* 13:76–80.
Phillips, P.
   1939   Introduction to the Archaeology of the Mississippi Valley. Ph.D. diss., Har-
          vard University.
   1970   *Archaeological Survey in the Lower Yazoo Basin, Mississippi 1949–1955.*
          Paper 60. Cambridge, Mass.: Peabody Museum of American Archaeology
          and Ethnology.
Phillips, P., J. Ford, and J. Griffin
   1951   *Archaeological Survey in the Lower Mississippi Alluvial Valley: 1940–1947.*
          Paper 25. Cambridge, Mass.: Peabody Museum of American Archaeology
          and Ethnology.
Pina Chan, R.
   1958   *Tlatilco.* 2 vols. Mexico City: Instituto Nacional de Anthropolgia e Historia.
Prigogine, I.
   1978   Time, Structure and Fluctuations. *Science* 291:777–85.
Quimby, G.
   1954   Cultural and Natural Areas before Kroeber. *American Antiquity* 19:318–19.
Radcliffe-Brown, A.
   1950   Introduction in A. Radcliffe-Brown and D. Forde, eds., *African Systems of
          Kinship and Marriage.* London: Oxford University Press.
Rathje, W.
   1971   The Origin and Development of Lowland Classic Maya Civilization. *Ameri-
          can Antiquity* 36:275–85.
Reeves, B.
   1973   The Concept of an Altithermal Cultural Hiatus in Northern Plains Prehistory.
          American Anthropologist 75:1221–253.
Rouse, I.
   1939   *Prehistory in Haiti: A Study in Method.* Publications in Anthropology 21.
          New Haven: Yale University.
   1958   The Inference of Migrations from Anthropological Evidence. In R. Thomp-
          son, ed., *Migrations in New World Culture History.* Tucson: University of
          Arizona Press.

Sanders, W.
1968 Hydraulic Agriculture, Economic Symbiosis, and the Evolution of States in Central Mexico. In B. Meggers, ed., *Anthropological Archaeology in the Americas*. Washington, D.C.: Anthropological Society of Washington.
Sanders, W., and B. Price
1968 *Mesoamerica: The Evolution of a Civilization*. New York: Random House.
Schneider, D.
1972 What Is Kinship All About? In P. Reining, ed., *Kinship Studies in the Morgan Centennial Year*. Washington, D.C.: Anthropological Society of Washington.
Schnell, F., V. Knight, and G. Schnell
1981 *Cemochechobee: Archaeology of a Mississippian Ceremonial Center on the Chattahoochee River*. Gainesville: University Presses of Florida.
Schoeninger, M., and C. Peebles
1980 Some Notes on the Relationship between Status and Diet at Moundville. *Southeastern Archaeological Conference Bulletin* 24:96–97.
Scott, S.
1981 Analysis and Interpretation of Faunal Remains from the Lubbub Creek Archaeological Locality. In C. Peebles, ed., Studies of the Material Remains from the Lubbub Creek Archaeological Locality: Prehistoric Agricultural Communities in West Central Alabama. Vol. 2. Report on file. Ann Arbor: Museum of Anthropology, University of Michigan.
Sears, W.
1954 The Sociopolitical Organization of Pre-Columbia Cultures on the Gulf Coastal Plain. *American Anthropologist* 56:339–46.
1977 Prehistoric Culture Areas and Culture Change on the Gulf Coastal Plain. In C. Cleland, ed., *For the Director: Research Essays in Honor of James B. Griffin*. Anthropological Papers 61. Ann Arbor: Museum of Anthropology, University of Michigan.
Sears, W., and J. B. Griffin
1950 Fiber-Tempered Pottery of the Southeast. In J. Griffin, ed., *Prehistoric Pottery of the Eastern United States*. Ann Arbor: Museum of Anthropology, University of Michigan.
Sellards, E.
1952 *Early Man in America*. Austin: University of Texas Press.
Service, E.
1975 *The Origins of the State and Civilization*. New York: Norton.
Severinghaus, C., and E. Cheatum
1956 Life and Times of the White-Tailed Deer. In W. Taylor, ed., *Deer of North America*. Harrisburg, Pa.: Stackpole Books.
Sheldon, C.
1974 The Mississippian-Historic Transition in Central Alabama. Ph.D. diss., Department of Anthropology, University of Oregon.
Skinner, M., and C. Kaiser
1947 The Fossil Bison of Alaska and Preliminary Revision of the Genus. *Bulletin of the American Museum of Natural History* 39:171.

Smith, B. D.
  1978 Variation in Mississippian Settlement Patterns. In B. D. Smith, ed., *Mississippian Settlement Patterns*. New York: Academic Press.
  1981 The Late Archaic-Poverty Point Steatite Trade Network in the Lower Mississippi Valley: Some Preliminary Observations. *Florida Anthropologist* 34:120–25.
  1985 Mississippian Patterns of Subsistence and Settlement. In R. Badger and L. Clayton, eds., *Alabama and the Borderlands: From Prehistory to Statehood*. University: University of Alabama Press.

Spaulding, A.
  1956 The Arzberger Site, Hughes County, South Dakota. Occasional Contributions 16. Ann Arbor: Museum of Anthropology, University of Michigan.

Stephenson, R.
  1954 Taxonomy and Chronology in the Central Plains-Middle Missouri River Area. *Plains Anthropologist* 1(1):12–21.

Steponaitis, V.
  1978 Some Preliminary Chronological and Technological Notes on Moundville Pottery. Paper presented at the 35th Annual Meeting of the Southeastern Archaeological Conference, Knoxville.

Steward, J.
  1938 *Basin-Plateau Aboriginal Socio-Political Groups*. Bulletin 120. Washington, D.C.: Bureau of American Ethnology.
  1955 *Theory of Culture Change*. Urbana: University of Illinois Press.

Stirling, M.
  1940 An Initial Series from Tres Zapotes, Vera Cruz, Mexico. Contributed Technical Papers 1. Washington, D.C.: National Geographic Society.

Stoltman, J.
  1972 The Late Archaic in the Savannah River Region. In R. Bullen and J. Stoltman, eds., Fiber-Tempered Pottery in the Southeastern United States and Northern Columbia: Its Origins, Context, and Significance. *Florida Anthropologist* 25(2):37–62.

Strong, W.
  1935 An Introduction To Nebraska Archeology. *Smithsonian Miscellaneous Collections* 93(19):1–323.
  1940 From History to Prehistory in the Northern Great Plains. *Smithsonian Miscellaneous Collections* 100:353–94.

Swenson, G., A. Anderson, W. Watkins, B. Williams, C. Launsbury, and R. Finley
  1941 *Soil Survey. Sumter County, Alabama*. Bureau of Plant Industry, Series 1935(18). Washington, D.C.: U.S. Department of Agriculture.

Taylor, W.
  1948 *A Study of Archaeology. Memoir Series of the American Anthropological Association* 69. Menasha.

Thomas, C.
  1898 *Introduction to the Study of North American Archaeology*. Cincinnati: Robert Clarke.

Thomas, D.
1973 An Empirical Test for Steward's Model of Great Basin Settlement Patterns. *American Antiquity* 38:155–76.
Toth, A.
1979 The Marksville Connection. In D. Brose and N. Greber, eds., *Hopewell Archaeology: The Chillicothe Conference.* Kent: Kent State University Press.
Trickey, B.
1971 A Chronological Framework for the Mobile Bay Region. *Journal of Alabama Archaeology* 17(2):115–28.
Trigger, B.
1963 Settlement as an Aspect of Iroquoian Adaptation at the Time of Contact. *American Anthropologist* 65:86–101.
1965 *History and Settlement in Lower Nubia.* Publications in Anthropology 69. New Haven: Yale University.
Tylor, E. B.
1871 *Primitive Culture.* London: J. Murray.
van der Leeuw, S.
1980 Analysis of Moundville Phase Ceramic Technology. *Southeastern Archaeological Conference Bulletin* 24:105–108.
1981 Ceramic Exchange and Manufacture: A Flow Structure Approach. In H. Howard and E. Morris, eds., *Production and Distribution: A Ceramic Viewpoint.* BAR International Series 120. Oxford, England.
1982 How Objective Can We Become. Some Reflections on the Nature of the Relationship between the Archaeologist, His Data, and His Interpretations. In A. Renfrew, M. Rowlands, and B. Segraves, eds., *Theory and Explanation in Archaeology.* New York: Academic Press.
Walthall, J.
1973 Copena: A Tennessee Valley Middle Woodland Culture. Ph.D. diss., Department of Anthropology, University of North Carolina.
1979 Hopewell and the Southern Heartland. In D. Brose and N. Greber, eds., *Hopewell Archaeology: The Chillicothe Conference.* Kent: Kent State University Press.
1980 *Prehistoric Indians of the Southeast: Archaeology of Alabama and the Middle South.* University: University of Alabama Press.
Walthall, J., and N. Jenkins
1976 The Gulf Formational Stage in Southeastern Prehistory. Memphis: *Southeastern Archaeological Conference Bulletin* 19:43–49.
Waring, A.
1968 The Refuge Site, Jasper County, South Carolina. In S. Williams, ed., *The Waring Papers, the Collected Works of Antonio J. Waring Jr.* Paper 48. Cambridge, Mass.: Peabody Museum of American Archaeology and Ethnology.
Waring, A., and P. Holder
1945 A Prehistoric Ceremonial Complex in the Southeastern United States. *American Anthropologist* 47:1–34.

Webb, C.
  1944 Stone Vessels from a Northeast Louisiana Site. *American Antiquity* 9: 380–94.
  1968 The Extent and Content of Poverty Point Culture. *American Antiquity* 33:105–14.
  1977 The Poverty Point Culture. In *Geoscience and Man* 17. Baton Rouge: School of Geoscience, Louisiana State University.
Webb, W., and D. DeJarnette
  1942 *An Archeological Survey of Pickwick Basin in the Adjacent Portions of the States of Alabama, Mississippi, and Tennessee.* Bulletin 129. Washington, D.C.: Bureau of American Ethnology.
  1948 *The Little Bear Creek Site, Ct8, Colbert County, Alabama.* Paper 26. University: Alabama Museum of Natural History.
Wedel, W.
  1936 *An Introduction to Pawnee Archeology.* Bulletin 112. Washington, D.C.: Bureau of American Ethnology.
  1959 *An Introduction to Kansas Archaeology.* Bulletin 174. Washington, D.C.: Bureau of American Ethnology.
  1961 *Prehistoric Man on the Great Plains.* Norman: University of Oklahoma Press.
  1964 The Great Plains. In J. Jennings and E. Norbeck, eds., *Prehistoric Man in the New World.* Chicago: University of Chicago Press.
  1978 The Prehistoric Plains. In J. Jennings, ed., *Ancient Native Americans.* San Francisco: Freeman.
Welch, P.
  1980 The West Jefferson Phase: Terminal Woodland Tribal Society in West Central Alabama. Paper presented at the 37th Annual Meeting of the Southeastern Archaeological Conference, New Orleans.
Willey, G.
  1945 Horizon Styles and Pottery Traditions in Peruvian Archaeology. *American Antiquity* 11:49–56.
  1949 Archeology of the Florida Gulf Coast. *Smithsonian Miscellaneous Collections.* 113:1–599.
  1966 *An Introduction to American Archaeology: North and Middle America.* Englewood Cliffs: Prentice-Hall.
  1971 *An Introduction to American Archaeology.* Vol. 2. Englewood Cliffs: Prentice-Hall.
Willey, G., and P. Phillips
  1958 *Method and Theory in American Archaeology.* Chicago: University of Chicago Press.
Willey, G. R., and J. A. Sabloff
  1974 *A History of American Archaeology.* San Francisco: Freeman.
Wimberly, S.
  1960 Indian Pottery from Clarke and Mobile County, Southern Alabama. Paper 36. University: Alabama Museum of Natural History.

Winters, H.
  1968   Value Systems and Trade Cycles of the Late Archaic in the Midwest. In L.
          Binford and S. Binford, eds., *New Perspectives in Archaeology*. Chicago:
          Aldine.
Wissler, C.
  1917   *The American Indian: An Introduction to the Anthropology of the New
          World*. New York: McMurtrie.
Wolf, E.
  1959   *Sons of the Shaking Earth*. Chicago: University of Chicago Press, Phoenix
          Books.
  1982   *Europe and the People without History*. Berkeley: University of California
          Press.
Wood, W., and B. McMillan, eds.
  1976   *Prehistoric Man and His Environments: A Case Study in the Ozark High-
          land*. New York: Academic Press.
Woodrick, A.
  1981   An Analysis of the Faunal Remains from the Gainesville Lake Area. *Bio-
          cultural Studies in the Gainesville Lake Area of the Tennessee-Tombigbee
          Waterway*. Vol. 4. Report of Investigations 14. University: Office of Archae-
          ological Research, University of Alabama.
Wormington, M.
  1957   *Ancient Man in North America*. 4th ed. Denver: Denver Museum of Natural
          History.
In Press *The Ancient Hunters and Gatherers of the Americas*. New York Academic
          Press.
Wynn, J., and J. Atkinson
  1976   Archaeology of the Okashua and Self Sites, Mississippi. Report on file.
          Starkville: Department of Anthropology, Mississippi State University.

Index

Primary forest efficiency, 119
Primary inhumation, 70
Processual view, 6
Projectile point, fluted, 22
Projectile point types:
—Flint Creek, 35
—Ledbetter, 33
—Little Bear Creek, 33
—Pickwick, 33
—Motley, 33
—Cotaco Creek, 33
—Wade, 33
Protohistoric, 20
Protohistoric simplification, 21

Rabbit, 76, 77, 94
Raccoon, 69, 76, 77, 94
Reeds, 100
Region: non-nuclear, 22; nuclear, 22
Reptiles, 52

Sage, 100
Saint Johns River, 36
Saint Louis, Missouri, 86
Saki-Chaha site, 47
Salt, 86
Scrapers, 94
Second-line resources, 69, 77, 80, 119
Sedge, 100
Seven Mile Island site, 102
Share, defined, 8
Shared, liberalized interpretation of, 8
Shell: beads, 80; bowls, 94; dippers, 94;
    gorgets, 94; hoe blades, 94; masks,
    94; pendants, 80
Shellfish, 41, 46, 52, 60, 76, 77, 119
Siblings, described, 107
Site 1Gr1 x 1, 67, 71, 73
Site 1Gr2, 46, 58, 60, 64, 67, 71, 73,
    100, 102
Site 1It563, 47
Site 1Lu59, 43
Site 1Pi33, 84
Site 1Pi61, 58, 67, 71, 73, 78
Site 22It563, 46
Site 22Le353, 61
Skull, 88
Skunk, 69
Slope forest, 39, 41, 42, 46
Social dynamism, 6

Social instrumentalities, 109
Social order: ranked, 24, 52; stratified, 24
Southern cult, 93, 97, 105
Spiro site, 86
Squash, 94
Squirrel, 41, 69, 76, 77, 94
Stable equilibrium, 35
State: conquest, 25; market, 25; trade, 25
States, absent north of Rio Grande, 20
Status, achieved, 125
Steatite, 33, 36, 37; quarries, 37; vessels,
    36, 37
Storage pits, used for burial, 80
Subject-object identity, problem of, 5
Succession to leadership, 129
Succession to title, disputes over, 127
Sumac, 67
Summer Haven site, 36
Summerville continuum, 91–92
Sun circles, 88
Superordination/subordination, 107–108
Surround, 23
Swastika, 88
Swords of chipped flint, 87
Syntheses: subregional with regional, 17;
    need for, 1; trends essential to, 2
System: external forces, 14; internal
    forces, 14
Systemic view, 13–16; problem of atom-
    ism, 14

Tallahatchie River, 116
Tallahatta quartzite, 33, 46
Taxa, composed of traits, 7
Taxon: aspect, summary of interpretation,
    104; component, summary of in-
    terpretation, 103–104; foci, summa-
    ry of interpretation, 103–104
Taxon horizons: as integrative taxon, 17;
    compatible with field of interaction,
    15; limited duration of, 15, 16; sum-
    mary of interpretation, 103–104;
    summary of proposed horizons, 104–
    106; as energy and matter exchange
    route, 15; Archaic interaction sphere
    as horizon, 15; Hopewell interaction
    sphere as horizon, 15, 49, 55, 105;
    Mississippian inconography spread
    as horizon, 89; southern cult as hori-
    zon, 93; steatite trade as horizon, 36,
    37, 104

About the Authors

Ned J. Jenkins is Park Manager and Archaeologist, Fort Toulouse/Jackson State Park. He received his B.A. and M.A. from The University of Alabama. This is his first book.

Richard A. Krause teaches anthropology at The University of Alabama. He received his B.A. and M.A. from The University of Nebraska and his Ph.D. from Yale University. He is author of *The Clay Sleeps: An Ethnoarchaeological Study of Three African Potters*.